Journey to Recovery

A Fifty Year History

Al-Anon   **Northern California**   Alateen

For information about Al-Anon in Northern California or to purchase additional copies of this book, write to

NCWSA
6426 Hidden Creek Drive
San Jose, CA 95120
http://www.ncwsa.org   info@ncwsa.org

Grateful acknowledgment is made for permission to reprint excerpts from copyrighted material published by Al-Anon Family Group Headquarters, Inc. Virginia Beach, VA 23454. Excerpts from the following publications were used in this publication.
First Steps Al-Anon…35 years of beginnings. © 1986.
1998-2000 Al-Anon/Alateen Service Manual © 1992.
Al-Anon Faces Alcoholism, Second Edition © 1965, 1984.
Al-Anon Family Group Forum, June, 1963 © 1963.
Digest of Al-Anon and Alateen Policies 1983 - 1985 © 1975.
Inside Al-Anon, Dec 1991 - Jan 1992 © 1991.
Inside Al-Anon, Aug - Sep, 1989 © 1989
Lois Remembers © 1979.

Grateful acknowledgment is made for permission to reprint excerpts from copyrighted material published by Alcoholics Anonymous World Services, Inc. New York, NY 10115. Excerpts from the following publications were used in this publication.
Alcoholics Anonymous Comes of Age © 1957, 1985.
Alcoholics Anonymous: The Original Manuscript July 1990. Purple Salamander Press, Reno, NV
Dr. Bob and the Good Oldtimers © 1980.
Pass It On © 1984.
A.A.World Services, Inc. requests that the following statement be printed in this publication.
"The Twelve Steps and Twelve Traditions and excerpts from A. A. literature are reprinted with permission of AA World Services, Inc. (AA W.S.) Permission to reprint the Twelve Steps and Twelve Traditions and excerpts from A A literature does not mean that AA W.S has reviewed or approved the contents of this publication, or that the AA W.S. necessarily agrees with the views expressed herein. AA is a program of recovery from alcoholism only— use of the Twelve Steps and Twelve Traditions and these excerpts in connection with programs and activities which are patterned after AA, but which address other problems, or in any other non-AA context, does not imply otherwise."

Roots of AA In Santa Clara County, not dated.
Children of the Healer © 1992 Hazelden Foundation, Center City, MN 55012-0176

ISBN 0-9706642-0-6
Publishers Cataloging in Publication
Title Journey To Recovery—a Fifty Year History of Al-Anon and Alateen in Northern California
    1. Alcoholism 2. Alcoholics—Family Relationships 3. Alcoholics—Rehabilitation 4. Adult Children of Alcoholics 5. Children of Alcoholics 7. Alcoholics—Spanish Family Members 8. Addiction 9. Abuse

Proposed by the Northern California World Service Committee in 1999.
Approved for distribution and sale at Al-Anon groups by the Northern California World Service Assembly September 9, 2000.

1 - 1500 - 01

Contents

Preface

No one individual knows the full history of Al-Anon as it grew in Northern California. Interviews, discussions, notes, letters, minutes, personal documents, newsletters were the sources of this *Journey to Recovery*. In addition to the tireless work of two volunteers, Irma C. and Art B., who did much of the research and actual placing of this book into its current form, there were several volunteers in the districts, information services and Intergroups who shared their own local history.

This is the story of those who began to believe that they could have recovery based on the model AA had given them. This is the story of how these men and women took certain steps to find recovery and how they met with each other in order to preserve what was successful and to discard what wasn't helpful.

From the earliest beginnings, most of the family members were women who wanted sobriety for their husbands. But in Northern California men were also seeking recovery from the beginning. It wasn't long after the groups received a letter from Lois W. and Anne B. that the few groups in California banded together to form their own Al-Anon Council. And they responded quickly to the needs of their own children and set up Alateen meetings.

These early members found that they needed to communicate with each other. So they formed regular business meetings in their communities as well as meeting area-wide three times each year at their Al-Anon Conferences.

Today, with 27 districts serving almost 800 groups, several Al-Anon Information Services and Intergroups, Literature Distribution Centers and a strong Assembly serving the area, current Al-Anon members are blessed not only with the assembly and conventions from the past that continue today, but they also have a strong area newsletter and several local newsletters and an electronic presence on the world wide web.

This history gives a chronological view of the growth of the area. In addition, there are chapters devoted to special parts of the Al-Anon program, notably Alateen, the Spanish contributions and those of special focused groups. Best of all are the variety of ways that our districts approached their services. The last half of this book is devoted to their history.

Nothing is complete when a history is written. We hope that you enjoy learning about Northern California Al-Anon roots, and recognize that it is possible to learn more by interviewing our long time members, even using this history to jog memories. We also hope that you will take the time to archive those things you have today: flyers of events, minutes of meetings, shares from speakers, so that the next generation will have as much material to describe the next chapter of the continuing improvements in Al-Anon and Alateen.

Acknowledgments

The history book committee wishes to acknowledge the special contributions of the staff of the Al-Anon Family Group Headquarters. We are especially thankful that the World Service Office made a strong commitment to preserve Al-Anon archives, publish historical literature, allow their archives staff to research specific items and for their willingness to allow the quotation of copyrighted materials relating to our area's history. We also wish to acknowledge the contributions of Alcoholics Anonymous World Services, Inc., who gave us permission to quote statements from their published books.

We are especially thankful to our Al-Anon and AA members who shared experiences with the writers and editors of those fellowships. We thank the many members who completed the Long Timer Questionnaires and shared information about how their groups began, how the meetings were conducted and what kept them coming back. This book would have been impossible to prepare without their significant contributions.

This history book was developed with the input of several members of Al-Anon, Alateen and AA. The NCWSA History Book Committee is grateful for those who provided information, reviewed the book for historical accuracy and gave helpful suggestions in editing and compiling this history.

Those listed here are known to have helped in some specific way. Irma C., Faun L., Mary A.-T., Peggy C., Art B., Cathy C., Past Delegates; Marilyn R., Delegate; Charli D., Kathleen D., Past Secretaries; Don R., Past Treasurer; Jennifer F., Alateen Coordinator; John C., Alternate Alateen Coordinator; Carol H., Past Area Archivist; Linda J., Alternate Area Archivist; Cathy F., Area Literature Coordinator; Alicia V., Amparo M., Esther G., Ruth S., Virginia T., and those who helped them, Hispanic Intergroup; Dottie J., Bobbie H., District 1; Lea L., Glenn S., Mary S., Nancy A., District 2; Sadi C., District 3; Marie D., Mary B., Sheilah K., Karen S., District 4; Richard K., Dick P., District 5; Amber E., George S., Max V. (Sacramento AIS), Bob J., Margaret H., District 7; Earthel N., District 8; Midge B., Colleen M., Galey S., District 11; Glynn D., Mary K., District 12; David B., Laurie R., District 13; Beverly A., Linda A., Ruth K., District 14; Olga, District 15; LaVonne O., District 16; Carol A., Debbie S., Delta D., Florence P., Jeanne E., Nancy N., Phyllis P., Randy M., Ruby, District 17; Deanna B., District 18; Beverly Anne S., District 19; Mark I., Santa Clara Valley Intergroup Archivist; Cathy F., Lynn G., District 22; Gail G., Gary S., Harlan H., Linda M., Stella, District 23; Kate M., Angela H., District 26; David R., Kathy G., District 27; John C. and John O'B., San Jose AA Archivists; Barbara M., Caryn J., Joe T. and Linda McF., Al-Anon Family Group Headquarters, Inc.; Gail LaC., AA Intergroup archivist, Akron, OH; and Bob S. Jr., Nocoma, TX, son of the co-founder of AA.

In addition, we also acknowledge those many unnamed and anonymous donors, who through their actions and their willingness to save documents, books and pamphlets and scraps of paper and to place them into the World Service Office, Area, District, AIS and Intergroup archives, have contributed greatly to the knowledge that has been used in creating this work of love.

1

Recovery for Early Relatives
of Alcoholics

"Damn your old meetings!" Lois W. once said. It's easy when we look through the rosy haze of fifty years of national and even international success of our recovery program to romanticize its beginning. It's also easy to lose the more inspiring picture of the human struggle that led to the birth of Al-Anon. When two alcoholics, Bill W. and Dr. Bob S., helped each other to remain sober and founded Alcoholics Anonymous, their wives understandably expected something other than what they got.

Lois W. was ecstatic that her husband was no longer drinking. His sobriety, however, didn't bring about the harmony and happiness at home that she expected. She was confused and other wives were experiencing the same confusion. Her husband was busy working with other alcoholics and frequently absent from home. Lois still provided the sole income for herself and her husband. She also supported many alcoholics in their home, doing the cooking and other household chores. There were no Al-Anon members ready to suggest that Lois put the focus on herself, and she didn't know that she needed to do that. "Even after Bill's spiritual awakening," Lois said, "it didn't occur to me that I needed to change."

Desperate wives were attending AA meetings with their husbands. AA originally allowed the wives to participate, and then allowed the wives to listen but not to speak, and called this an open meeting. As time went on, AA began to understand that alcoholics would achieve recovery and maintain it only if the groups had a single purpose. The wives were relegated to the kitchen to serve coffee and snacks. The women needed help themselves, so Annie S., Lois W., Anne B. and other wives set out to create Al-Anon for themselves. Annie S., Dr. Bob's wife, understood that the philosophy used by the sobering alcoholics could apply to the wives, but she died before the movement had a name. Lois, nearing retirement in 1951 and recovering from a heart attack, reluctantly accepted the duty placed on her by her husband.

In California, Mrs. Kellogg of Monterey purchased the first AA Big Book delivered to California for her husband in 1939. She was desperate for her husband to become sober. It was in Long Beach, CA in early 1941 that the first non-alcoholic group formed. This group wrote an opening and closing for their group, which today is part of the pamphlet *This is Al-Anon*[1]. Shortly after the San Francisco Auxiliary of AA was formed, Ruth G. established a newsletter for the wives. According to Lois W., this newsletter, the *Family Forum*, was instrumental in establishing a presence for non-alcoholic recovery throughout the United States and several other countries.

The foresight of the wives in California surged throughout the world. This chapter devotes itself to describing how the alcoholics began recovering in Northern California, and especially how the wives gradually went from glowing in the recovery of their husbands to realizing that they were still unhappy. This is how the non-alcoholic groups began in Northern California and how they contributed to the structure that eventually became known as Al-Anon Family Groups.

Before the Beginning

The history of alcoholism spans the centuries and probably caused relationship problems from the first time someone drank the fermented juice of a fruit or berry. In the earliest days of our country's heritage, Temperance societies became advocates of moderation and even abstinence from liquids containing alcohol. Bill W.[2] wrote of the importance of the Washingtonian movement[3] that began in the 1840's. This society first focused on helping alcoholics, and later took on other causes. In the 1870's, Carrie Nation became infamous for her raids on and destruction of the bars in her community. In 1919, the US Federal Government attempted to prevent alcoholism by passing the 18th Amendment[4] to the Constitution[5], which banned the manufacture and sale of intoxicating liquors.

The Oxford Group

In the early 1920's Dr. Frank Buchman[6] founded a society called the Oxford Group[7] for the express purpose of applying first century Christianity to modern day life. Rowland H.[8] turned to the Oxford Group after his treatment by the psychiatrist, Dr Carl Jung.[9] It was Dr. Jung, who said that psychiatry had no understanding of how to help an alcoholic achieve sobriety, but that he was aware of a few alcoholics who stayed sober after having received a "spiritual experience". It was Rowland who helped Ebby T.[10] get sober using the Oxford Group principles. It was Ebby who approached Bill W. in the fall of 1934. Shortly afterwards, Bill had what he called a spiritual conversion experience and never drank again.

Lois W.[11] was ecstatic when her husband finally stopped drinking. It is obvious from her writings that she loved her husband throughout her life. Lois always said how good a man he was, if only he could stop drinking. She now thought her problems would be over. She said, "I shared Bill's gratitude for what the group had done for him and for so many other people, people I surmised must have had grievous problems of one sort or another. My only problem, Bill's drinking, was being solved, so I felt no personal need for their teachings. I was only too glad to help them, but for nearly a year it never occurred to me to apply the program to myself." [12]

In Akron Ohio, Mr. Firestone[13] spent much of his personal efforts and resources to achieve sobriety for his son, unsuccessfully. On a trip to the West Coast, the son met a member of the Oxford Group and came home sober with his new friend. Grateful, Mr. Firestone asked Dr. Buchman to establish a group in Akron. Many of the executives of the various tire companies, including the Seiberlings[14], were invited to join this group. Frank Seiberling's daughter-in-law Henrietta joined and soon encouraged her friends, Dr. Bob S. and his wife Annie, to join. Dr. Bob[15] was a reluctant visitor, but Annie S. accepted these Oxford principles in her own daily life. Annie continued her resolve to help Dr. Bob conquer his drinking habit.

Bill W. meets Dr. Bob S. and Annie S.

In the spring of 1935, Annie S. and Henrietta Seiberling[16]convinced Dr. Bob to make a confession of his weakness at the Oxford Group meeting. Only a few weeks later, Bill W. went to Akron on a business trip[17]. When the business purpose failed, he found himself in the Mayflower hotel with only $10.00 in his pocket and no hope of obtaining more funds to return home. Torn between the bar and making a phone call, Bill W. called Reverend Tunks[18] and was given several phone numbers. He called Henrietta Sieberling. He asked her if she knew an alcoholic to whom he could speak. Henrietta had been praying for someone to help Dr. Bob, and was very excited by Bill's phone call.

Dr. Bob S. and his wife Annie invited Bill W. to their home. Within the month, Dr. Bob no longer drank. The two of them were determined that the experience they had shared could be duplicated with other alcoholics. Bill W. stayed several months. During that time, he and Dr. Bob made their first attempts to help Bill D.[19] quit drinking. Annie S. invited his family to stay with them.

Annie S. contributes to recovery for non-alcoholic wives

Annie S. had an early understanding of the importance of the whole family achieving recovery, not just that of the alcoholic. She articulated the Oxford Group principles to the wives in ways they could understand. She spoke of detachment, surrender to God's will, anonymity, equality of members. She practiced prayer and meditation and avoided criticism. Annie S.'s work with families of alcoholics was the forerunner of what would become Al-Anon Family Groups. In a letter[20] to Bill W., Henrietta D.[21] acknowledges that Annie S. formed the first group. She said, "In the early part of 1936 Annie organized a 'woman's group' for wives of alcoholics, whereby in her loving way, she tried to teach us patience, love and unselfishness."

Sober alcoholics continued to find their recovery until early 1937, when the New York contingent broke away from the Oxford Group. In Akron, the whole family was encouraged to attend Oxford Group meetings. It was after 1939 that the early alcoholics in Akron split from the Oxford Group, but family support continued to be very important. In fact, an early draft of the AA Twelfth Step was as follows, "we tried to carry this message to others, especially alcoholics"[22]. When the book *Alcoholics Anonymous* was printed, the words were changed to "we tried to carry this message to alcoholics." The alcoholics realized that they needed a single purpose, alcoholics helping other alcoholics, in order for their fellowship to survive. This change would eventually prove significant to the family members. They realized the need to meet separately to support each other, while still encouraging the alcoholic to stay sober. Annie S. died in 1949, leaving the burden of organizing the unconnected non-alcoholic groups to a reluctant Lois W.

Lois W. shares about the period from 1934 to 1950 in her Memoirs

Lois said in her memoirs[23], "I was not as happy as I should have been after all my dreams of Bill's sobriety had come true…I felt left out and unneeded. Even after Bill's spiritual awakening, it didn't occur to me that I needed to change. One Sunday Bill casually said to me, 'we'll have to hurry or we'll be late for the Oxford Group meeting.' I had a shoe in my hand, and before I knew what was happening I had thrown it at him and said, 'Damn your old meetings.' That day, I began to look at myself analytically for the first time. Ever since the shoe throwing incident, I have taken a daily inventory and tried to be honest with myself, to analyze my thoughts and feelings as objectively as possible."[24] Lois' outburst wasn't because Bill was drinking—he was sober. Lois wasn't receiving attention from Bill, the alcoholics in her home were. She was the only breadwinner and was still cooking and cleaning up after all these people. She learned she was full of self-pity because they had no life together.

"Annie S. had belonged to the Oxford Group[25] before we met her and had felt the need for her own spiritual growth, as I did after the shoe-throwing incident. So whenever we met with the wives of other AAs, we each told them how we had come to the decision to live by the same principles as our mates."

"It wasn't until 1940, however, that constructive gatherings for the families of AAs began to evolve.…At first, we either played bridge or gossiped, but soon we began to discuss our own problems and what we could do about them. I told my story. It was great to find that because others had gone through similar experiences,

A letter carried by Bob S. Jr.

Bob S. holds dear to his heart the virtues that his mother Annie S. held as her husband struggled to recover from the disease of alcoholism. Henrietta D. wrote this letter to Bill W. on the occasion of the death of Annie S. in 1949. Bob S. Jr. carries this letter with him and often quotes it when he speaks to Al-Anon and AA audiences.

On Friday, June 28th, 1935 I met Ann Smith. I met Doctor Bob on Thursday morning in the hospital. On Thursday evening I went to the hospital to see my husband. Dr. Bob was there and he said, "The little woman would like you to come over to the house." I told him I couldn't go that night but would go the next night. On Friday night when I went to the house on Ardmore Avenue, I met the most thoughtful, understanding person I have ever known. After talking with her for a while, I addressed her as Mrs. Smith and she said, "Ann, to you my dear." She wanted to remove all barriers. She wanted God to have full credit for this wonderful thing that had happened to her. Bill W. was there at this time. After they talked with me for a while, Ann asked me if I would like to "go all the way with God." I told her I would. She said we should kneel, which we all did, and told me to surrender myself to God and ask Him, if he had a plan for me to reveal it to me.

Ann taught me to have a "quiet time" in the morning that I might feel near to God and receive strength for the day. She taught me to surrender my husband to God and not to try to tell him how to stay sober as I tried that and failed. Ann taught me to love everyone. She said, "Ask yourself, what is wrong with me today if I don't love you?" She said "the love of God is triangular—it must flow from God through me—through you—and back to God."

She told me I should never criticize the remarks of the person leading the meeting as we do not know God's plan. Maybe what that person says will meet the need of someone in the group.

In the early part of 1936 Ann organized a "woman's group" for wives of alcoholics, whereby in her loving way, she tried to teach us patience, love and unselfishness. Ann made it plain to me from the beginning that she wanted no credit for herself; it was God. All she wanted was to keep herself so she could know and follow God's plan.

When I met and talked with this intelligent and deeply spiritual woman, I was completely sold on AA.

(Signed) *Henrietta D_ _ _ _ _*

each of us no longer had to be alone with our troubles. Our family gatherings were composed mostly of AA wives, with a sprinkling of mothers and daughters. There was one man, Wally S., a father who was trying to get his son into AA.

"Probably few present-day Al-Anon members ever heard of Ruth G.[25], but without her early involvement, Al-Anon could never have gained the impetus it did. In 1949, she started a small 12 page monthly magazine called *The Family Forum*[26] for discussion of family problems arising from alcoholism. Its pumpkin-colored sheets were filled with editorials, correspondence from families of alcoholics, appropriate quotations from the Bible, Marcus Aurelius Antonius, St. Francis of Assisi, Nietzsche, ancient Chinese philosophers, and even Machiavelli."

Lois W. wrote about Annie S. "Annie's part in the formation of AA and consequently in the foundation of Al-Anon should never be forgotten, especially by Family Group members. Although there were few family groups during the thirteen years of her activities, Annie did much to instill the spirit of Al-Anon in many of the families of alcoholics." Bill W. gratefully acknowledged her contribution at her memorial service in 1949, calling her "the mother of AA."

Lois continues to share[27], "In 1950, Bill went by himself to the AA groups to find out their feelings about establishing a General Service Conference for AA. **He was surprised to run into so many family groups.**" Bill suggested that Lois open a service office "where these groups could register, receive helpful literature and become more unified."

National Publicity for Alcoholics Anonymous

An article titled "Alcoholics and God"[28] in the September 30, 1939 issue of *Liberty*[29] magazine was responsible for early inquiries from the San Francisco Bay Area to the Alcoholic Foundation[30] in New York City. While living in Monterey, Mrs. Kellogg, whose husband drank too much, purchased the first copy of the "big book," *Alcoholics Anonymous* sold in Northern California.

Formation of Alcoholics Anonymous in Northern California

Two alcoholics formed a group in Oakland and met for the first time in April 1941. In a letter[31] to the Alcoholic Foundation, the group secretary described their progress, "Our meetings take place at the Oakland Y.M.C.A. every Monday evening with a membership of approximately fifty persons. Attendance averages from 30 to 40. On the last Monday of the month we hold an 'open meeting' for members and their families and friends, with an attendance of about 120."

In June 1941, in a letter[32] from the secretary of the Sacramento Group, the wife of an alcoholic is described this way. "Pauline C. is as you say a grand person. The poor girl had a very tough row to hoe as her nerves are shot. Her husband is a mighty fine understanding chap and has stood by her like a brick. Needless to say, he feels more than repaid for the change that the association with AA has made in their lives." By September, there were AA groups already formed in Sacramento, San Francisco, San Jose, Oakland and Palo Alto.

In another letter[33] to the Alcoholic foundation, Henry K. says, "Please let me drop a line to say that I am happy today and sober and my wife does not complain of nervousness nor headaches."

The Oakland Group gave its "annual report" of the group's activities. This letter describes how Pauline G., a non-alcoholic, was elected the secretary. "Besides offering consolation and sympathy where needed, her home is open to members at any time."

Bill W. and Lois W. Visit the Bay Area

In 1943, expressing concern about traveling too far, Bill W. wrote[34] to the Palo Alto Group and gave his schedule to "arrive at San Francisco November 24th and leave December 4th for Portland and Seattle....Besides, I ought to think about Mrs. Wilson. To a degree this will be a vacation for her." They spent the Thanksgiving weekend with members of the Palo Alto group.

Lois had a different view of this same trip. "On the trip Bill and I took in 1943 to visit AA groups, I usually spoke briefly at the large open meetings... But at teas and luncheons for the families, I tried to make more personal talks, telling how important it was for me to live by the spiritual principles of AA... At San Francisco, there were eighty-five wives on hand to hear me tell my story."[35]

In 1944, the San Jose AA Group wrote[36] to Bill and Lois about an open meeting. "Ricardo is out on parole you know. He is really a master. A fine chap. Making the most wonderful talks all over. We held a glorious open meeting here in San Jose in his[37] honor. His debut as it were. It was marvelous; we had three judges who praised the movement highly and two teachers from the bible institute. The adult probation officer and dozens of wives, also new faces. About 100 all told."

The Salinas AA Group formed in February 1944. By 1948, there were four AA groups in San Jose.

Early participation of non-alcoholic wives in Northern California

By 1945, AA had formed groups in Oakland, Sacramento, San Francisco, San Jose, Palo Alto and Salinas. At all of these meetings, non-alcoholics were present and participating. At the Oakland Group, a non-alcoholic wife even became the group secretary. But these roles were only supporting roles aimed at helping the alcoholic stay sober. In September 1945, the San Francisco AA Group formed an auxiliary for families and friends. In a reply[38] to Ruth G.'s letter to the *AA Grapevine*, the Alcoholic Foundation said, "We were glad to get news of the San Francisco Family Club, founded in September, 1945. While these associate AA groups do not register in usual sense of the word, we attempt to keep a record of information regarding their plan, methods of procedure and other pertinent data... I imagine you are familiar with the pamphlet put out by the group in Long Beach, California."

Three additional non-alcoholic groups attempted to register with the Alcoholic Foundation in 1949 and 1950, each choosing a unique name. The Berkeley Group was formed in March 1949, and called itself the "Adeline Nalano Group." Ruth C., the secretary, offered her home at 2831 Dohr St. where the group met every other Monday. In November 1949, the Nalano Group was formed in Sacramento, where Floyd G. was the first secretary. In October 1950, the San Jose group called itself the Alano-Mrs Group. It had fifty members and met on San Carlos St. The first secretary was Melba W., and Gerrie R. became the next secretary.

How Al-Anon Family Groups began

"Bill's suggestion, to form a separate society for non-alcoholics, did not appeal to me at first,"[39] said Lois, but she was intrigued by the thought. A neighbor, another Anne, Anne B., had started a family group nearby, and volunteered to help Lois. After consulting with wives of the AA delegates at the 1951 General Service Conference, the two women wrote to the 87 groups that were listed at the AA office. Of these 87, the four listed above were from Northern California. In their letter, Lois W. and Anne B. suggested the purpose of the groups might be

1. To give cooperation and understanding to the AA at home.
2. To live by the 12 Steps ourselves in order to grow spiritually along with our AA.
3. To welcome and give comfort to the families of the new AAs.

They also asked two questions,

1. Do you approve the name AA Family Group? If not, what do you suggest?
2. Should we not accept the 12 Steps as written for AA, without change or embellishment?

Help for families of alcoholics was finally becoming a purpose for these non-alcoholic meetings. In all those years of support, Annie S., first articulated the idea that the families might need help. Support for wives of alcoholics generated spontaneously throughout Northern California, the United States and the rest of the world. Lois, though initially reluctant, poured her heart and soul into establishing a unity for these groups that paralleled the structure of Alcoholics Anonymous. The next chapters describe how the wives of alcoholics banded together in Northern California and helped to develop the fellowship they eventually agreed to call Al-Anon Family Groups.

Notes

[1] *This Is Al-Anon*, P-32 is available from AFG Headquarters, Inc.

[2] Bill W. is a co-founder of Alcoholics Anonymous.

[3] *Pass It On*, p 367, *Twelve Steps and Traditions*, p 178. Published by AA World Services.

[4] Prohibition was ended when the 18th Amendment was repealed on December 5, 1933 upon the ratification of the 21st Amendment to the Constitution.

[5] *Webster's Universal Unabridged Dictionary*, page xiii.

[6] Dr Frank Buchman was a Lutheran minister who founded and led the Oxford Group movement for at least two decades. The Oxford Group was nondenominational and based on the four absolutes: absolute honesty, absolute unselfishness, absolute purity and absolute love.

[7] In 1936, the Oxford Group "reached its height of popularity as an inspirational movement."

[8] Rowland H. from "a prominent Rhode Island family, mill owners," found sobriety in the Oxford Group. *Pass It On*, p 114, publisher, Alcoholics Anonymous World Services, Inc, 1984.

[9] Dr. Carl Jung practiced psychiatry in Switzerland. This is where Rowland first attempted to become sober.

[10] Ebby T. became Bill W.'s sponsor. Ebby never achieved long-term sobriety, but did find sobriety shortly before his death in the early 1960's.

[11] Lois W., along with her neighbor Anne B., eventually co-founded Al-Anon Family Groups

[12] *Lois Remembers*, P 91. Reprinted with permission of Al-Anon Family Group Headquarters, Inc.

[13] Mr. Firestone was the founder and president of the Firestone Tire and Rubber Company.

[14] Frank Seiberling was "the entrepreneur who had built the Goodyear Tire Company" and "later formed the tire company bearing his name." From *Pass It On*, p 136, © 1984. Reprinted with permission of Alcoholics Anonymous World Services, Inc.

[15] Dr Bob S. was a prominent surgeon in Akron, OH with a drinking problem.

[16] Henrietta was the daughter-in-law of Frank Seiberling, part of the Goodyear rubber family, and an active member of the Oxford Group.

[17] Bill W. was working to collect proxies in order to gain control of the National Rubber Machinery Corporation.

[18] Dr. Walter Tunks, the pastor of the Episcopal church in Akron.

[19] An attorney, Bill D. was the first alcoholic in Akron to achieve continuous sobriety with the help of Bill W. and Dr. Bob.

[20] This letter is in the possession of Bob S., the son of Dr. Bob. Reprinted with permission of Bob Smith.

[21] Henrietta D. is the wife of Bill D.

[22] *Alcoholics Anonymous*, Original Manuscript, p 27. Reprinted with permission of Alcoholics Anonymous World Services, Inc.

[23] *Lois Remembers*, pages 172-173. Reprinted with permission of Al-Anon Family Group Headquarters, Inc.

[24] *Lois Remembers*, p 98-100. Reprinted with permission of Al-Anon Family Group Headquarters, Inc.

[25] Ruth G. was the secretary of the San Francisco Family Club.

[26] Originally called the *Family Club Chronicle*, the *Family Forum* had a circulation of 1,200 and was distributed to Australia, South Africa, as well as to most states. In 1954, Ruth gave the rights to the name to AFG Headquarters. *The FORUM* continues to be published by AFG today.

[27] *Lois Remembers*, pages 173. Reprinted with permission of Al-Anon Family Group Headquarters, Inc.

[28] The subtitle is as follows: "Is there hope for habitual drunkards? A cure that borders on the miraculous—and it works!"

[29] *Roots of AA in Santa Clara County*. Reprinted with permission of the publisher.

[30] The organizers of AA founded the Alcoholic Foundation on August 11, 1938. It later became Alcoholics Anonymous World Services.

[31] This letter, dated September 25, 1941, is the earliest description of the efforts of help for families of alcoholics in Northern California.

[32] This letter, dated June 13, 1941, was written to the Secretary of the Alcoholic Foundation to let them know that their second meeting occurred the previous night and that they had 8 members.

[33] Dated December 6, 1941, Henry wrote to let the foundation know of the progress of the meeting.

[34] The letter is in response to Dave's request that Bill W. attend the Palo Alto Group when traveling to the West Coast.

[35] *Lois Remembers*, p 172. Reprinted with permission of Al-Anon Family Group Headquarters, Inc.

[36] Letter written on March 15, 1944, was from the group secretary whose address was the Montgomery Hotel.

[37] The meeting was in honor of Dr. Cutler, who was working with inmates at the correctional facilities in California.

[38] This letter, dated August 17, 1950 is found in *First Steps*, page 26. Reprinted with permission of Al-Anon Family Group Headquarters, Inc.

[39] *Lois Remembers*, pages 173-174. Reprinted with permission of Al-Anon Family Group Headquarters, Inc.

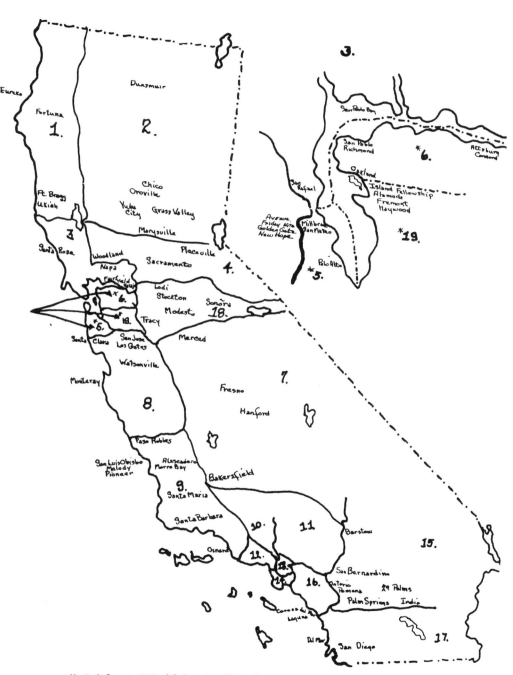

All California World Service Districts
January 1, 1963

2

The Area's First Twenty Years

In May 1951, Lois W. and Anne B. wrote a letter to all the known non-alcoholic groups. This letter is the historical first that began the process of organizing the separate groups from around the country into a cohesive organization. After they received replies from many of the groups, the volunteers headed by Lois and Anne, and several AA members concluded that a separate organization founded on the same principles as those of AA was necessary. In 1952, in Northern California the groups were coming to the same conclusion. A meeting was called at the AA Council conference. "All non-alcoholics at the AA conference interested in doing something for themselves will meet in the auditorium on Saturday at noon" was how George S. remembered the notice on the hotel bulletin board. Those early participants agreed that there was a need to organize locally so that they could more efficiently carry the message to those families who needed help. They formed the Al-Anon Council and met at the same time as the AA Council. It took almost ten years for Al-Anon's national organization to begin connecting to the groups through a system of delegate conferences similar to those of AA. A local assembly was formed in the early 1960's and the Council continued to co-exist with the assembly. The council continued to plan conferences. The assembly met at these conferences, usually on Saturday morning. The assembly distributed a newsletter and planned the events that would acquaint the professionals, doctors, nurses, schoolteachers and law enforcement about the recovery now possible from the effects of alcohol on the family. They elected trusted servants, established districts and informed the public. The groups in Northern California grew from 11 groups to several hundred. Finally in 1970, the council and the assembly combined their treasury. In 1971, the area assembly became responsible for all functions at the area level.

At the Beginning

The four "wives' groups" in Northern California received the letter from Lois W. and Anne B. The purpose of this yet unnamed organization was to establish a Clearing House[1] to preserve the unity of Al-Anon by coordinating its message. The letter[2] presented the idea of a worldwide organization and a name for the organization. They found that groups were using a variety of names and various forms of the Steps. There is no written record of how the four Northern California groups voted, or even if they responded. It is probable that some of them did, because of the 87 letters mailed to the groups, 48 replied to the Clearing House in NY.

On November 17, 1951[3], at a meeting in New York, Lois W., Anne B. and the other volunteers reviewed the replies from the groups. It was at this meeting that the name, Al-Anon Family Groups, was chosen after several AA members objected to the use of AA as part of the new organization's name. Over the years several members have wondered why the "-" appears in Al-Anon. These minutes of the meeting mention two AA clubhouses in New York. One of them is called the Alanon Club. A later publication[4] states that the "-" appears to avoid confusion with these clubs. In her memoirs, Lois W. writes, "The word Al-Anon is simply a derivative of Alcoholics Anonymous, combining the first syllables of each word."[5] Lois wrote in relation to the Steps, "We sent a memorandum to AA asking permission to use its Twelve Steps in our Fellowship. AA agreed unofficially, but its members felt strongly that we should be a separate society, and not a subsidiary of Alcoholics Anonymous. In addition, Bill felt AA's should hold no office in our structure. He often said, "Keep us drunks out of it."[6] At a later meeting in March 1952, the volunteers noted that several groups had adopted various versions of the Steps and concluded that the groups recognized the power of the Steps of AA. They adopted the Steps of AA as the Al-Anon guidelines, changing only the word "alcoholics" to "others" in the Twelfth Step.

By 1950, the AA groups had 15 years of forming and working together when the AA members accepted the AA Traditions at their first International Convention in Cleveland. In July 1952, Lois began working on a similar set of guidelines for Al-Anon that would be effective for the rapidly growing Al-Anon Family Groups. In her early drafts of the Traditions, she used the words "separate entity" and "cooperation with Alcoholics Anonymous" to assure that Al-Anon and AA are separate and have different purposes. In early 1953, Lois W. drafted a letter to the AA delegates and the Al-Anon groups. Her letter asked the groups and the AA delegates whether they would accept the Traditions for Al-Anon as presented. The number of groups who responded was low, but four groups from the area, the San Jose Group, the Alameda Group[7], the Marysville Nalano Group[8] and the Sacramento Group[9], voted to accept the Traditions as presented in her letter. The Al-Anon Traditions were ratified at the next AA International Convention in 1955 and reaffirmed by the Al-Anon delegates at the first Al-Anon World Service Conference[10] in 1961.

Organizing the Area

At the Northern California Conference of Alcoholics Anonymous in San Rafael in February 1952, representatives of these early groups formed the Al-Anon Northern California Council. George S. of Sacramento reflects on that first meeting, "A note appeared on the bulletin board stating that all non-alcoholics at the AA conference interested in doing something for themselves were to meet in the auditorium on Saturday at noon. I told my wife that if another man were there, I would stay. There were 50 women and two men. I met Andy from Oakland. We elected a committee of seven members. I was chairman and Andy was vice-chairman. We had a secretary and treasurer too. Then we all went home. By telephone and letter, we worked up a program for the June 1952 Conference in Santa Rosa. The Al-Anon schedule was printed on the back of the AA program."

By the end of 1952, there were already 11 Al-Anon groups listed with the Clearing House. These groups met in Berkeley, Eureka, Fresno, Modesto, Monterey, Napa, Roseville, Sacramento, Salinas, San Francisco and San Jose.

Vivien F. of San Rafael reports about the June 1953 Al-Anon Conference. "Great strides were taken by the Al-Anon Council since its inception less than 12 months previous. She reports that a very fine program has been scheduled for their meeting in Vallejo. For the first time the sessions will be extended into a period covering two days. This will allow the non-alcoholics to have their time occupied while the alcoholic mates are busy in their meetings."[11]

The Al-Anon program at this conference is credited to George S., of Yuba City, a member of the Marysville Al-Anon Group, Jim and Peggy L. of Vallejo and George of Santa Rosa. Mary J. of Sacramento was the speaker, Marge M., also of Sacramento, moderated several group discussions, and Alice B. of Roseville gave a report on Al-Anon activities at the AA General Service Conference[12] in New York.

The Al-Anon Northern California Council tried a delegate[13] system in the 1950's. The delegate system was patterned after the successful organization of AA. From the council handbook[14] we find the following statements:

> Benefiting from prior trial and error and utilizing all past experiences, the present Delegate System of the Northern California Council of Al-Anon was presented to each group in Northern California with the request that they approve or disapprove by either sending a delegate or a written expression[15] to the Conference. As a result of these procedures, the present Delegate System was adopted at the Fresno Conference in March 1960.

The purpose of this council is defined as: "The Northern California Council of Al-Anon acts as a medium of exchange between member groups for the dissemination of ideas and experiences of mutual interest, and provides whatever other services those member groups may deem advisable. One of the important functions of the Council is to plan the agenda for all Northern California Conferences. The Northern California Conferences of Al-Anon are held in conjunction with AA's Northern California Conferences. These Conferences convene three times a year in various locations throughout Northern California. The Conference provides a place for Al-Anon members all over Northern California to assemble and participate in meetings pertaining to all facets of the Al-Anon program, such as: World Service, Northern California Council, Alateen, various types of workshops and panel meetings, as well as speaker meetings. The Conference makes it possible for us to carry the message of Al-Anon to the public as well as at the grass roots level, in all areas."

Development of the Area Assembly

In 1960, the Al-Anon Family Group Headquarters[16] requested that certain states and provinces from the United States and Canada send a delegate in 1961 to New York to attend an Al-Anon World Service Conference[17] annually for three years as an experiment. This conference followed the structure of AA, except that AA had selected a term of two years rather than the three years Al-Anon had selected. California responded and elected a delegate to the World Service Conference, Helen B., and an area chairman, Al S., who were both from Southern California.

In May 1962, the California World Service Assembly noted that there was little participation by the groups from Northern California. They recognized that costs of travel might have been a factor, though one person commented that if groups set aside just ten cents a day, there would be sufficient funds to attend the assembly in Southern California. As a result, the assembly decided to hold its 1962 meeting in San Francisco. They also decided that the alternate delegate should come from the North and elected Ann O. as the first alternate delegate. While the delegate herself opposed the division of California along the lines of AA's boundaries, she brought the petition to divide California into two areas to the 1963 World Service Conference at the request of the Northern California groups. "Those who attended the Northern California Committeeman and Group Representative Meeting in Modesto, Saturday, May 18, heard our state delegate, Helen B., give her report of the results of the annual Al-Anon 1963 World Service Conference, held in New York City in April and heard that at this, the 3rd Conference of its type, our request for two separate Assemblies in California had been approved effective January 1964."

The Northern California Al-Anon committeemen and group representatives met to begin the process of establishing a separate assembly at its meeting on May 18, 1963 in Modesto. At the August 1963 meeting, they outlined a map of the new districts[18]. The old District # 8 was divided and renamed Districts XI and XII. District XI consisted of Palo Alto, Santa Clara, San Jose and Saratoga, and District XII consisted of Watsonville, Monterey, Pacific Grove, Salinas and Santa Cruz. The minutes reflect, "This is considered a better plan from an operational viewpoint as it more closely follows AA's organization with the result that the existing homogeneous area feelings are enhanced and transportation problems of mates to the various functions are somewhat reduced."[19]

The members of this meeting also planned for their first election assembly with a request that all groups elect a group representative and an alternate. According to the minutes, this assembly was held during the regular Fall AA Northern California Conference at the 3,000-seat auditorium of the Berkeley High School in Berkeley. In fact while the AA Conference held its meetings in the auditorium, the Al-Anon assembly was in a much smaller room in the high school. During the assembly they elected a delegate, Ann O., assembly Officers, including the chairperson, John F., Secretary, Virginia C. and Treasurer, Emylee M. Two coordinator positions were established, the Map Committee, chaired by Alice S. and the News Editor, headed by Emylee M. John F. wrote a report for District 8, ending it with a special poem.

> Many of us lose confidence in prayer because we don't recognize the answers:
> We ask for strength and God gives us difficulties, which make us strong.
> We pray for wisdom and God sends problems, the solution of which develops wisdom.
> We plead for prosperity and God gives us brain and brawn to work.
> We plead for courage and the Lord gives us dangers to overcome.
> We ask for favors and God gives us opportunities.

The line that divides California into two areas was drawn from west to east along the county borders separating Kings County and San Luis Obispo County. The counties east of the Sierra Nevada mountain range were placed in the Southern area because these towns along highway 395 could more easily access meetings in the south. The 1964 assembly map shows the area divided into 12 districts. This map shows that district II[20] has eight groups and encompasses the area from Highway 80 to the California-Oregon border. The *1964 World Service Office Meeting Directory* listed a total of 69 groups in Northern California.

After the 1963 assembly, groups continued to elect both a Northern California Council delegate, who met to plan the Al-Anon program at the tri-annual Northern California AA Conferences and a group representative. From 1964 to 1970, the assembly and the Northern California Council each operated independently, even though they both met at the same conference. Within the assembly structure, the delegate depended on the area committee, which consisted of the area officers and district committeemen[21] to find out how things were progressing in the districts and to discuss ways to carry the message. Setting up a service structure of officers, committeemen and group representatives was an important task. Members began to realize that aside from attending meetings, they were being asked to volunteer their service beyond the group level so that the area would grow. During this period, the World Service Conference and the assembly were new and many Al-Anon members were not even aware that the assembly existed. In 1971, the council and assembly voted to merge. The council's funds were transferred to the assembly. At this time, the name chosen for the assembly was "Northern California World Service Area" (NCWSA). As John F., the first area chairperson explained, "There is a lot of leg work to do if you want to perpetuate Al-Anon." A past delegate shared, "Many members were content to attend their meetings and still are. They didn't understand why it was necessary to spend a Saturday driving to and from an out-of-town service meeting and spending time away from their family. But we embraced this new thing called service."

Conferences and Conventions

The Northern California Al-Anon Council held three conferences in conjunction with the AA Conferences from 1952 until 1971. After the Al-Anon Council merged with the assembly, the assembly continued to meet at the same time and place as the council conferences until 1978. The NCCAA selected nine cities and towns throughout Northern California. The Al-Anon committee also hosted their own program of recovery in addition to the committee meeting. When they first began, Al-Anon meetings were held in a single room, and the assembly meeting was held on Saturday morning. The Al-Anon portion of the conference would schedule a luncheon speaker. There were no separate Al-Anon meetings when the AA speaker shared. Typically AA speaker meetings were held on Friday night, Saturday night and Sunday morning. Beginning in 1979, assemblies were no longer held at the NCCAA Conferences, but the area committee continued to meet on Saturday until 1993.

Newsletters

Newsletters have been a vital means of communications since the beginning of Al-Anon in Northern California. The Non-Alcoholic Family Group of the San Francisco Fellowship of Alcoholics Anonymous began publishing a monthly newsletter, *The Family Club Chronicle* in July 1950[22]. This group changed the name of their monthly newsletter to the *Family Forum* in May 1951. At that time they had a mailing list of about 1,200 that included most states and several countries, including Canada, South Africa and Australia. In 1954, when the Ruth G., the editor, stopped publishing the newsletter, Lois W. requested and received permission to use the name, *Family Forum* for the World Service Office newsletter. The Clearing House had its own Newsletter called *Newsletter* beginning in 1952 and changed its name to *The Family Group Forum* in 1956. Thus today's *FORUM* has its roots in our own area.

The Northern California Council Handbook states: "The Alternate Secretary shall act as news reporter for our N.C.C., making sure that news about our Conference is placed in *GOOD NEWS*, both before and after the Conference." This became the second newsletter in Northern California and provided information of interest to Al-Anon members and groups.

In 1964, the delegate began the practice of writing to all the groups when necessary. By 1970, the official newsletter of the assembly, was conceived, named and edited by Irma C. As late as 1978, it continued to be a single 8 1/2'" x 14" sheet of paper folded in two, appearing as four pages. For many years the *12 Stepper* included a logo that included a staircase. On each step, a stick figure, carrying a letter appeared. The figures were obviously wounded at the first step and obviously well at the last step.

Literature

Wives' groups in other areas wrote their own pamphlets. After the Al-Anon Clearing House was formed, the groups offered these pamphlets for publication. Lois and Anne also wrote several pamphlets, such as *Information for the Newcomer*[23] and also wrote the book, *Al-Anon Family Groups*[24]. Northern California members learned about recovery from using this literature. Even so, most long-time members don't remember using any literature at early meetings. One member, when asked what they used, said, "We didn't have all this literature that is available today. We concentrated on learning the meaning of the words in the steps. We also did a lot of 'loving interchange,' where we shared with each other about how to help the alcoholic stay sober."

Ray C., an early member from San Jose, related that when he visited the 1970 AA International Convention in Florida, Lois expressed the need for a pamphlet for men. On the way home, he and two other men from San Jose agreed to write some material and then consolidate it into a single sharing. After the three completed their combined sharing, they sent it to Lois W. in New York. When Ray went to the 1975 International AA Convention in Denver, he visited the literature table and picked up all the literature he didn't have at home. While he was returning home, he read the pamphlet, *Al-Anon is for Men*[25]. He recognized the sharing as the one he and his companions had sent to Lois five years earlier.

Committees and Coordinators

Committees have also played an important part in the development of the NCWSA structure. The Al-Anon Northern California Council had a Hospital and Institutions chairman, one of whose duties was listed as follows: "The H & I Chairman should have a working knowledge of H & I meetings from actual attendance and interest, in order to create interest among others in this type of activity." In 1964, two new coordinators were appointed. Alice S. headed the Map Committee and Emylee M. was the News Editor. By 1970, there were also Alateen and Public Relations coordinators.

Finances

During the delegate terms of Ann O. (1964-1966) and Muriel B., (1967-1969), the council received donations from the conferences, groups and members. It paid its expenses and then distributed surplus funds using a formula to send one-third to the World Service Office, one-third to AA and keeping one-third for their own expenses. The one-third to AA was in lieu of payment of rent and other expenses of the Northern California Council Conferences. Since most of the donations came at the conference, this was done at the three conferences each year. In 1971, total revenue of NCWSA was $2,107 and expenses $2,205, with an ending balance of $847, which includes a balance from 1970.

Growth of Groups

In 1952, the first *World Group Directory of Al-Anon Family Groups*[26] from the Clearing House listed 27 Al-Anon Family Groups in California, 11 of which are in NCWSA's existing boundaries. The 1964 directory listed 218 groups in California. That year in Northern California, there were 69 Al-Anon groups, six Alateen groups, one Intergroup in San Francisco, and one lone member in Napa. Shortly after the new boundaries were decided, the southern boundary of District II were changed so that those groups in Auburn and Grass Valley could attend district meetings in Sacramento, which was easier for them rather than going to the north towards Chico.

By 1939, 100 alcoholics had become sober and we can presume that many of their wives were also part of their recovery. In 1951, when Al-Anon was organized, the early family members already knew and used the AA principles, especially the Steps, in their own lives. It was easy for them to accept the Steps as their own, with just the word "alcoholics" changed to "others" in the Twelfth Step. In 1953, with two years of study of how AA used their Traditions, Al-Anon groups adopted their own Traditions based on the 12 Traditions of AA.

This period of time was one of learning what the role of alcoholism played in the family. Northern California began with one non-alcoholic group as part of an AA group in 1945, grew to four in 1951, 69 in 1964 and over 200 in 1970. By 1971, all the basics of the Al-Anon organization were in place. The Steps of Alcoholics Anonymous were in use for thirty-two years and the Traditions of AA were in place for 21 years. Even the Twelve Concepts of AA were in use and accepted by AA for nine years. Minor changes were made to the Traditions until 1961 when the first World Service Conference approved them for the last time. And in 1970, Al-Anon adopted its own Twelve Concepts of Service. Now the foundation was in place. The largest growth of Al-Anon was still ahead.

Notes

[1] The Clearing House was located in the 24th Street Clubhouse. First Steps, p 50.

[2] The letter is printed in *Lois Remembers*, page 173, © 1979 and in *First Steps*, p 43 © 1986, Al-Anon Family Group Headquarters, Inc.

[3] The name, "Al-Anon Family Groups" appears on a letterhead with this date, in *First Steps*, p 50.

[4] This was mentioned in the November 1987 issue of the *FORUM*, published by AFG Headquarters, Inc.

[5] *Lois Remembers*, page 176. Reprinted with permission of Al-Anon Family Group Headquarters, Inc.

[6] *Lois Remembers*, page 176. Reprinted with permission of Al-Anon Family Group Headquarters, Inc.

[7] The response was received on 17 February 1953.

[8] They responded on 31 March 1953.

[9] This group responded on 4 April 1953. *First Steps*, p 83.

[10] This Conference is described as Al-Anon's largest worldwide group conscience.

[11] *First Steps*, P 47. Reprinted with permission of Al-Anon Family Group Headquarters, Inc.

[12] It was often the wife of the AA delegate who attended the AA General Service Conference activities.

[13] The "delegate" was the group's representative to the Council meetings, giving input to the planning of the Al-Anon program at the conference.

[14] The Northern California Council published this handbook some time after 1960.

[15] Proxy voting (voting by mail) is no longer allowed at the assembly.

[16] Al-Anon Family Group Headquarters, Inc became the official name of the Al-Anon Clearing House when it became incorporated in 1954. *First Steps*, p 159.

[17] The members elected each year are called a Panel. Panel 1 was elected in 1961. In 2001, the Panel number is 41.

[18] The new 1963 map of Northern California districts is after chapter 1, p. 11.

[19] Minutes dated August 21, 1963 in NCWSA Archives.

[20] District II covered the interior of CA from Highway 80 to the California-Oregon border. One group met in two cities, Mt. Shasta and Dunsmuir.

[21] Al-Anon originally adopted the same title used by AA. Later the title was changed to district representative.

[22] *First Steps*, p 24.

[23] *Information for the Newcomer*, S-4, is published by AFG Headquarters, Inc.

[24] Al-Anon Family Group Headquarters, Inc. published *The Al-Anon Family Groups* in 1955. The name was changed to *Living With an Alcoholic* when the book was expanded in 1962. There were two substantial revisions, in 1968 and 1978. In 2000, AFG Headquarters republished the original text as *The Al-Anon Family Groups*, with the subtitle *Classic Edition*.

[25] The pamphlet, *Al-Anon is For Men*, P-1, was completely rewritten by AFG Headquarters in 1999.

[26] The 1952 World Group Directory of Al-Anon Family Groups is shown in *First Steps*, pages 72 and 73.

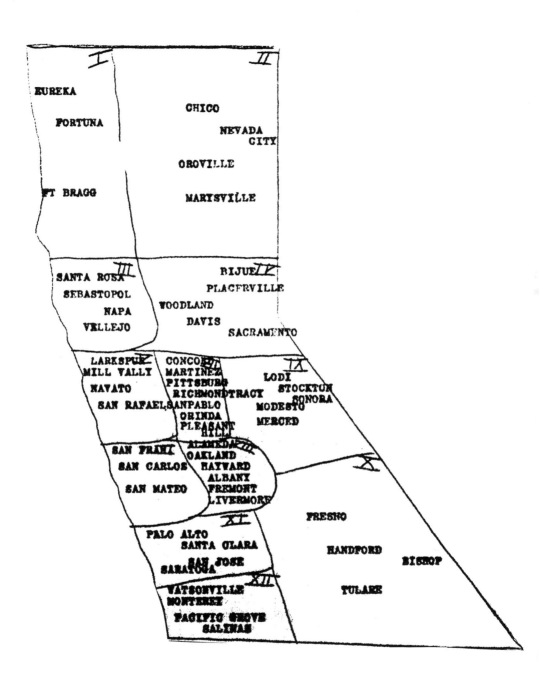

Northern California World Service Districts I to XII
1964

3

The Next Thirty Years

By 1970, the Al-Anon World Service Conference had met ten times. They had developed procedures for describing the purpose of Al-Anon, for unifying the message to the public, for development of Conference Approved Literature and a host of services to the groups, most of which continue today. Books available included *Living With an Alcoholic, Al-Anon Faces Alcoholism*[1] and *One Day At a Time in Al-Anon.*[2] By 1973, the experiences of the Al-Anon groups in working with each other were compiled into a service handbook[3]. The area brought together their two organizations into one, began serving the public with their outreach to the communities, the newcomers with meetings opening in every small and large community and the members with excellent conventions and conferences.

Members in Northern California developed their functions from an organization that "served cookies and cakes at AA functions" to learning about how to recover using the 12 Steps and how to relate to other groups through the Traditions. In 1970, the two area committees, the Northern California Al-Anon Council and the assembly merged because there would be "less bookkeeping and both committees served the same purpose". The council was mostly involved in assuring that the Al-Anon message was being delivered at conferences and in local public information. The assembly was mostly involved in helping the delegate when she went to World Service Conferences and in trying to implement the new ideas that came back to the area. The World Service Conference even changed the names of the "district committeeman" to that of "district representative" at their 1971 conference.

The purpose in Tradition five "to help families of alcoholics" became more alive to these early pioneers. They were about to see the number of Al-Anon groups in Northern California grow from fewer than 200 groups to over 1,000 in the next twenty years. Then in the last ten years, growth stalled and the number of Al-Anon and Alateen groups actually declined about 20%. The assembly and the districts coped with a new set of circumstances and dealt with maintaining enthusiasm in a new environment of uncertainty. This chapter identifies the wonderful things they learned and some of the hardships that occurred as a result of the efforts of this remarkable volunteer organization.

The 1970's

As the 1970's began, there were still very few documents to help these trusted servants coordinate, compare notes and come to agreements. The members met at three Al-Anon conferences held as part of the NCCAA Conference. The area assembly was held here on Saturday mornings from 9:00 to 11:00 AM. This was the forum for discussing how to carry the message of recovery to others. Members shared the conflicts, concerns, successes and conflicts at this forum. The phrase, "talk to each other, reason things out" was often used. But, as Irma C. shared, "There were clashes of opinions. Individuals who could not accept the majority vote of the assembly or the area committee began writing letters to officers, the *12 Stepper* editor and others. Copies of the letters were sent the World Service Office (WSO) Policy Committee and the Board of Trustees." These letters continued and around 1974, one letter asked the WSO how to remove a delegate from office. "The alternate delegate, with the help of many past officers and two past delegates, read a 'paper' to ask the group representatives for a vote of confidence in all officers because all the officers stood behind Bonnie H. The vote of confidence was given with tumultuous applause."

In 1973, the assembly voted that the alternate delegate also serve as the chair of the Conference Planning committee. Prior to this era, the wife of the AA speaker was usually the Al-Anon speaker. This practice changed as Faun L. developed a speakers' list so that the conference could choose its own Al-Anon speaker. Money was budgeted to bring a speaker each year from outside the area. Alateens held one open and one closed meeting during the conference. An Alateen Sponsors Workshop was also held on Sunday morning prior to the Spiritual Speaker's meeting.

At the June 1975 assembly meeting in Oakland, Faun L., the area secretary, began audio taping the assembly meetings to be able to better transcribe minutes when she returned to her home. A committee also developed guidelines to reimburse the expenses for the coordinators and committee chairmen.

The expenses of the World Service Conference, attended each year by the delegate, were paid from an "equalized expense" fund, where part of the funds were paid by the WSO from group contributions and the remainder, $460.00, paid by each area was approved. Because the delegate had to travel an extra day from the west coast, the delegate's personal expense fund used to attend the World Service Conference was increased to $200.00 plus the regular expenses. Irma C. presented the assembly with a new map of the district borders, and the assembly voted to reimburse her for the costs incurred. She also reported that the annual subscription rate for the *12 Stepper* is $1.30. Bonnie H. brought questions that would be decided at the next World Service Conference. Both were about litera-ture. "Should the pamphlet, *How to Know an Alcoholic*[4] be continued on the litera-ture list; and should the cover of *Alcoholism, A Merry Go-Round Named Denial*[5] be changed to conform to Conference Approved Literature?" She also asked, "Is your group registered with New York?"

Members participated in the Pacific Regional AA Service Assembly[6] (PRAASA), then held in May, to hear the delegate's World Service Conference report. As a result, the assembly voted to pay part of the delegate's expenses to PRAASA by the providing the expenses of the airline ticket.

In October 1977, an incident in Santa Rosa showed how much the two fel-lowships had grown. The Al-Anon assembly usually met on Saturday morning from 9:30 to 11:30 AM. Two AA members interrupted the meeting at 11:15 and demanded that the Al-Anon business meeting "had to go." Nearly 100 Al-Anon members protested loudly to no avail. Irma C, the delegate-chairman, tried to stand on the base of a lamp post in the conference center parking lot so the audi-ence could see and hear her. They concluded the rest of their business before lunch.

Several practices existed at the area conferences, many of which continue to-day. It was traditional that the Al-Anon committee be responsible for the Saturday luncheon and that Al-Anon provide a speaker. Hilarious skits became more popu-lar and more were added. AA members continued to tape the conference speakers, including the Al-Anon speakers. Bill, Tillie's husband from Modesto, was the first taper. Bart D. continued with the practice when Bill died. After Bart's death in 1993, Terry D. became responsible for the NCCAA tape library, a post he contin-ues to hold.

With *Pebbles in the Pond*[7] in 1976, the WSO developed new Public Informa-tion pieces, which helped the area. A TV network, PBS, broadcast the Carol Burnett film, *Drink, Drank, Drunk*. It included a tag line with Al-Anon public Informa-tion phone numbers that brought many to members to Al-Anon. Readers Digest published *An Oasis Called Al-Anon*. The WSO Public Information booth was sent to the California Personnel and Guidance Association Convention in San Fran-cisco, and later for the Orthopsychiatric Association Convention. Al-Anon mem-bers manned the booths, passed out literature and spoke with several interested persons. One counselor said, "I don't know what you do in Al-Anon, but please keep doing it! When I can't get anywhere with an alcoholic client, I just send the rest of the family to Al-Anon and Alateen. That takes care of it!"

In 1978, the group representatives noted that it was too costly for the GRs to attend three assemblies each year. The assembly voted "that we have an annual meeting on a Saturday in February to conduct all business, hear from GRs, DRs, coordinators and liaison members."[8] During the next year, many assembly func-tions were delegated to the NCWSC committee, which continued to meet three times each year at the AA conferences. The assembly also voted to eliminate the "pink cans" that were used to fund individual area services and established a gen-eral fund for all services. They formed a budget committee composed of the cur-rent treasurer, a past treasurer and one other person who was appointed by the delegate-chairman. An early financial report reported that 30 groups and one district had contributed $699.73. In 1978, 250 people attended the Monterey Conference and 70 attended the World Service Day in Chico. At the end of 1978, the balance on hand was $1,655.93. As the area completed the decade of the 1970's, the treasurer reported the annual financial report. Groups contributed $5,220. Revenue from three conferences and the World Service day provided the balance. In addition to registration, revenue came from the 7th Tradition basket, the luncheon, literature sales, raffles and a coffee kitty.

Many new groups were now forming and many of them weren't registered with either the WSO or with the area. At the time, groups would register with the WSO first. Then when the area secretary received the WSO roster, she would add the groups to her own list. In the meantime, the *12 Stepper* Editor was receiving group addresses that didn't agree with the WSO or the area lists. The *12 Stepper* was changing into a communications forum from the area committee members, including the district representatives and intergroups, as well as the officers, delegate and coordinators. Because this newsletter now was the chief source of information from NCWSA, the area sent a free copy to all groups.

The 1980's

The Al-Anon committee began to plan Saturday night meetings at the AA conferences, though it was previously customary for Al-Anon members to attend the Saturday night AA Speaker meeting. "Society was changing, to include divorcees, singles, sisters, brothers, parents etc."

When Faun L. was elected as delegate in 1979, she accepted the position with a request that the assembly elect a separate assembly chairperson. Lois B. was elected and chaired the February 1980 Assembly in Modesto, attended by 87 group representatives and 12 district representatives. They voted that the next assembly be a two-day assembly.

In 1982, assembly divided and renumbered the districts, voted to establish committee guidelines, to incorporate and to support the Al-Anon portion of the AA Hospitals and Institutions Conference. The assembly assigned a new task to the alternate delegate, that of budget chair, and that an Archives Coordinator be appointed to collect and preserve archival materials. A Bylaws committee was appointed and the area received both non-profit status with the IRS and incorporation with the state. Several guidelines were put into place, including those for the area conference and the Area World Service Committee. Later in the decade, the Alateen Sponsor Guidelines were put into place. When the World Service Office began holding Regional Service Seminars[9] (RSS), the assembly approved a motion that the delegate could attend either the RSS or PRAASA. Later on, they removed the approval to attend PRAASA and approved sending three area members, the delegate, alternate delegate and the chairperson, to the RSS when it was held in the Southwest region. They later modified their motion to allow other officers to attend if any of those authorized to do so were unable to attend. In 1976, the Southwest Regional Delegates Meeting[10] (SWRDM) was formed to allow current and past delegates assist new delegates in learning what they needed for attendance at the World Service Conference. Gradually, the assembly approved the payment of expenses to send all the past area delegates to this meeting. Later, when the SWRDM allowed other participants, the alternate delegate and the chairperson were also authorized to attend.

For the first time since its incorporation in 1954, the WSO Board of Trustees reached out to Northern California for a board member. Irma C. was selected through the regional process and served as a trustee from 1982 through 1984.

In 1989, the treasurer announced at the October NCWSC committee meeting that groups had stopped sending in funds to support NCWSA. He believed it to be temporary, suggesting that the emergency appeal letter sent by the WSO in August might have cleaned out the group treasuries. Instead of panicking, the committee held two workshops, each one with a different question. How can we maintain services with reduced funds? How can we increase services while using the same amount of funds? One result of this exercise was that the committee voted to reduce its mileage allowance from $0.20 per mile to $0.10. The immediate result of this decision was to reduce NCWSA expenses by $1,500. This turned out to be the year that the number of meetings of Al-Anon peaked. Locally, NCWSA had about 1,000 registered groups and there were 33,000 Al-Anon and Alateen groups worldwide.

The 1990's

As the 1990's began, group members saw the need for an area prudent reserve to avoid the problems that occurred in 1989. One was established with $7,500 as the starting amount. The budget committee was charged with adding $1,500 each year when funds were available. The total to be placed into this reserve was determined to be one-half year of the area's expenses. The fund could only be used with a vote of the assembly. By 2000, the fund has grown to about $16,000, not quite a half-year's expense yet. Several times during the past ten years, the fund was used when either the expenses were higher than usual or donations were less than expected.

In 1990, there were still three conferences held each year along side of the NCCAA Conferences. Both the NCCAA and Al-Anon groups were much larger and it was difficult to find conference centers big enough for both the AA and the Al-Anon Conference. In 1993, the assembly decided to hold an annual Convention independently of NCCAA. This convention began the following year and is held by rotation through the area's three sections. Districts within the hosting section bid on the event and are often full participants in the planning and execution of the convention. In addition to English Speaking and Alateen portions of the convention, the Spanish community also plans a full slate of service and recovery topics at this convention.

Delegates share their experiences

Mary A. T. shared her experiences as delegate from 1988 through 1990 in the *12 Stepper*. This was some of her thoughts. "One hope I have for my first year as delegate is that we keep in mind the quality of service we each employ. I anticipate healthy differences of opinion and interpretation and equally healthy problem-solving efforts together. Unity comes about not so much by a united mass consciousness but by an informed group conscience. We will conquer personality problems by recognizing and appreciating that principles will prevail. I will stay over one day at the World Service Conference to make my one and only trip to Stepping Stones, where delegates have the opportunity to meet Lois W. Lois Wilson died on October 5, 1988 at the age of 97.

"Thanks to Marilyn R. for arranging a very inexpensive round trip ticket to the SWRSS. We had a lot of fun listening to the flight attendants and pilots as they delivered their spiel through their two Dixie cups and a string! The information presented at the Southwest Regional Delegates Meeting is invaluable to new and returning delegates."

In July 1989, Mary presented a letter from the World Service Office. The letter explained how the financial situation at the WSO prevented them from holding a separate International Conference in San Diego, as was done in Montreal and Seattle. Instead they recommended that Al-Anon ask AA to subsidize the program as was done in earlier years.

In December 1989, Mary reports her visits to districts, including sharing at the Spanish Speaking All-State Convention. "You have accomplished a lot, for it begins with each member of a group and carries through an upward journey, rather than being handed down. Work within your personal program to discover what you can do, within the principles of our program. Your voices and viewpoints are valuable, hard and often acted upon. When it seems that this isn't true, remember the seed was planted and may need time to germinate."

In July 1990, Mary reported, "Service is part of our 12-Step work of trying to carry the message. Service is exciting. It is sometimes tedious. It calls on us to truly learn the meaning of principles before personalities. Our personal growth and our spiritual growth blossom." And in August, "In regard to Alateen meetings for those 12 and under, I didn't sense any opposition to such meetings being formed as long as teaching doesn't happen and as long as it is the Alateen member who instigates the formation of the meetings. The WSO is not enthusiastic about such meetings, since the potential to develop into a babysitting or class room exists."

Peggy C. shared about her experiences during her term from 1991 to 1993. "I saw disagreements at the conference without being disagreeable and realizing with awe that much is getting done, when you could swear that nothing is getting done. The literature committee reports that a piece on 'growing up with alcoholism' will include sharings from members under 12 years of age. Spanish services reports that there is an overwhelming growth of Al-Anon groups in the US. This supports the projections that the Hispanic community is the fastest growing minority in this country. The forum on Al-Anon's financial future demonstrated the concerns felt by all in the fellowship."

In August 1991: "Worldwide Al-Anon is going through a non-growth period right now and needs your input on how to cut expenses and how we can enhance our public image." In April 1992: The WSO sent a letter to every group in appreciation of increased contributions in 1991."

July 1992: "Have you ever walked through a crisis and felt an overwhelming sense of gratitude for sponsors, sponsees, prayers, principles and the support of family and friends? I look around me and am saddened by what I see—petty squabbles, power struggles, inflated egos, impatience and intolerance—not just in the world at large, but in our own area and my local district. I also see many of us sincerely seeking spiritual solutions trying to place principles above personalities, remembering that in place of trying to force solutions, that the Al-Anon program tells me I can seek a solution. I can carry the message of recovery. I can live the program of recovery."

In August 1992: "During the WSC conference an earthquake struck Eureka and riots broke out in Los Angeles. The California delegates were then known as the 'movers and shakers'. After mentioning the area's Alateen Sponsorship Guidelines, I mailed them to 28 delegates who asked for them."

April 1993: "Over the years, I have found service work to be a catalyst for a great deal of personal growth. It has taught me to place principles above personalities. Most of all service work keeps me teachable. In every position others told me I was not alone and that I don't have to do everything all by myself. Do I really care if Al-Anon is here for the next bunch of newcomers? Am I willing to take the time to fulfill this commitment? If the answer is 'Yes', then Let It Begin With Me!"

June 1993: "It is with a great joy to announce that our past delegate, Mary A.-T., has been elected as Southwest Regional Trustee to the WSO Board of Directors."

December 1993: "You have congratulated me when a job was well done, and you have called me on it at those times when my character defects were hanging out all over the place. But the best part is that you loved me and let me know it through all of it. Believe me, there's always a need to be filled and the rewards far outweigh the workload."

Art B. shared, "During my term as delegate, 1994 to 1996, the World Service Conference tackled several difficult issues. Al-Anon was unable to continue to support increasing rents in New York City in the face of declining numbers of groups and donations. An ad hoc committee had been formed to find a new location outside of large cities. After examining over 300 locations throughout the US by computer, winnowing the number to 50 and then 4, the ad hoc committee visited the cities of Palm Beach, FL; Dayton, OH; Virginia Beach, VA; and Greenville, SC. The first three were similar in size and the last was a significantly smaller city. The cost of services, salaries and availability of Al-Anon members as volunteers were some of the criteria used in making their final decision. The World Service Conference supported the final decision to move the Al-Anon Headquarters to Virginia Beach, VA.

"The next decision was whether to lease again or to purchase a building for Al-Anon exclusive use. I asked for input from our Al-Anon members, read all I could about the topic in both AA and Al-Anon literature, consulted with many individuals, including a respected AA member. I personally came to the conclusion that there were no statements in our Traditions that prevented an Al-Anon service board from purchasing property for their own use. But there were still questions that many had placed with me. I brought them to the World Service Conference. The deliberation had no time limit. We discussed, asked, thought and questioned the board chairman for 8 hours. At 10:30 PM, we prayed silently, said the Serenity Prayer and voted. The conference overwhelmingly agreed with the proposal to purchase the property, manage it in a separate committee and to make the final decision in fifteen years from 1996.

"The result has so far been positive. The cost of rent, close to $1 million in New York City in 1994 is now less than $300,000. The use of a separate committee of Al-Anon members with experience in real estate has removed the day-to-day management of the building from the hands of WSO staff, which frees them to focus on helping families of alcoholics."

Cathy C. shared, "When serving as your delegate, I was one of the many links of service in our area and for our program during the years of 1997-1999. My primary responsibility was to attend the World Service Conference, share their message with you and share your message and my experience with them. I was able to listen at many district meetings and assemblies as the group representatives shared about their groups' progress and area coordinators shared about their outreach projects. This is one of the ways the delegate learns about the area's issues and concerns. We do have so much recovery in those rooms! The three World Service Conference themes were 'Communications—Our Hope for the Future,' 'Inventory—Searching for Progress and Growth,' and 'Carrying the Message—Our Primary Purpose.'

"The most exciting news during my term was the opening of new World Service Office in Virginia Beach, VA. Your contributions built a new modern building, which uses the Al-Anon logo as the decorating theme. Ten of the 55 employees in New York City moved to Virginia Beach. The new service structure trial period began too. The learning curve was tremendous that first year as everyone from the Executive Director to the warehouse men were in new positions, learning new jobs. What a joy it was to tour the office and meet our employees in Group Services, Membership Outreach, Fellowship Communications, Public Outreach and Business Services. The Archives room stores our history safely. The Translation department proudly displays our literature in twenty-three different languages. The free 800 number phone lines are ringing with inquiries for help from prospective members and professionals. The print shop is humming with activity as new and revised pamphlets are printed, collated, cut and stapled. Every day, the truck pulls away from the warehouse dock with shipments of books and pamphlets going to individuals, groups and literature depots.

"The two major steps with Conference Approved Literature were the release of *Paths to Recovery*[11] in 1997 and *Having Had A Spiritual Awakening*[12] in 1998.

The World Service Office began an inventory of the available literature. The first year, our area reviewed the pamphlets *Alcoholism, The Family Disease*[13] and *Alateen Talks Back on Detachment*[14]. We learned that *Alcoholism, The Family Disease* was one of our original booklets and was written before Al-Anon was incorporated in 1954. The Preteen group that critiqued *Alateen Talks Back on Detachment* reminded us that their parents do not appreciate when their children 'Talk Back.' We recommended that the title of the series be changed. The second year, because of our support and activity with Alateen, we inventoried *A Guide to Alateen Sponsorship—An Unforgettable Adventure*[15]. Our Alateen sponsors felt validated and supported by this book. No major changes were recommended to this book. *The Dilemma of an Alcoholic Marriage*[16] was the 1999 assignment. Many thought the title could be changed to *Dilemma of an Alcoholic Relationship.*[17] Also, those reviewing the book thought it could be combined with the *Sexual Intimacy and the Alcoholic Relationship*[18] booklet. These suggestions were forwarded to the World Service Office for their consideration.

"In 1998, our area invented Diversity Day[19] to address the multiple cultures and communities in Northern California. The Spanish members helped us understand the differences and similarities in carrying our message of hope to these new members. The Institution Conference expanded their horizons to include this new subject by sharing their conference space for the second Diversity Day in 1999. Now, the World Service Office is recommending that other areas follow our example and host Diversity Days too!

"During my term, technological advances were made. First, the Northern California Website was created and implemented. It contains general information about our program as well as a calendar of events, a list of over 600 meetings, and information about Conference Approved Literature. It linked with many other websites so a newcomer is helped in many ways. We assisted other areas with establishing their websites. Second, our group records were improved by receiving a disk from the World Service Office with our 800+ groups listed. District representatives and the Group Records Coordinator worked diligently to update the groups' addresses and contacts for the World Service Office and our database. Last, I participated in the delegates email group called DOL. Experience, strength and hope are shared as well as general information, area practices, guidelines and personal updates. It was a strong support for me during my term and as I transition from being the current delegate to being a past delegate.

"The important personal lesson I learned was the importance of conserving energy and resting. I learned more about my physical and mental limitations. Also, for the first time in my life, the house I live in became a special safe home during my term as delegate. Yes, service definitely was putting my program into practice and learning to recover with others with love. What tremendous gifts we have received!!"

Marilyn R., the new Panel 40 delegate in 2000, shared the importance of bringing problems and questions to her attention so she could participate in the

Chosen Agenda Items[20] section of the World Service Conference. The questions chosen for discussion at this conference were:

1. What is the best method of getting and keeping new members?
2. How do we carry the message to all who suffer from this disease?
3. How do we implement the new WSO structure within our own areas?
4. What is the best way to encourage volunteers for service work?

She reported the activities that are planned for Al-Anon's 50th anniversary as an organization. The highlight for the World Service Office will be a celebration dinner at the end of the 2001 World Service Conference. "This was such an overwhelming experience," she said.

Group Records

The group roster was originally typed on plain white paper, listing the groups, district by district. Phoebe, the NCWSA Recording Secretary, would give Irma C. the list for the *12 Stepper.* "Group representatives would also give me their group addresses," Irma said. "These were often not listed on the roster Phoebe had given me. So—we had a two-way effort. There were a little more than 200 groups in 1970. In 1976 when I gave up editing the *12 Stepper,* the number of groups was 'pushing' 500."

An early Group Records Coordinator shares, "Beverly M., the editor of the *12 Stepper,* phoned me to ask if I would help with an Al-Anon newsletter. Bev came over to my house one day and spread the bits and pieces of the newsletter on my dining room table. I remember asking Bev how many she needed to mail, expecting her to say a number less than 100, and instead, hearing her say something like 'I don't know, maybe 700 or so.' I happened to be involved in another organization in Martinez. Betty Beeman, a member of that organization, had just volunteered to create mailing labels for that organization—not just type them, but create a database and print them from a Xerox 820, a dedicated word processor. So I asked Bev if Al-Anon would be interested a database for us. I would design the database, Betty would do the data entry at home and print labels for us for $.01 a label."

This was the start of the database system. NCWSA eventually purchased its first piece of office equipment in 1987, a Xerox computer and database software called "Q & A." In the mid 1990's another Group Records Secretary, Ari T.-F., proposed that the records be updated to a Microsoft Access database. She also worked with the group records person at the World Service Office, so that the fields in both the WSO and NCWSA databases would match where appropriate. This led to the WSO sending out their Northern California records as a Word document and their accepting changes from the area in the same electronic form so that the area and WSO records would match.

NCWSA Incorporation

In 1981, during one of the NCWSC meetings, a member shared a newspaper article about two of the AA Southern California Literature Depots being served with an outstanding tax bill for thousands of dollars in back taxes. The article indicated that the IRS would be auditing other 12 step organizations, since they sold literature and other miscellaneous items. During the next year, the pros and cons were discussed extensively at committee meetings. Some of the reasons the area decided to incorporate were: 1) we didn't want to break the law, so, if it was necessary to pay taxes, we were prepared to do so; 2) we felt our treasury was too big for just a resale permit and 3) we wanted to protect our trusted servants from lawsuits. In February 1982, the assembly agreed that NCWSA should incorporate.

Cathy C., Daly City, was appointed chair of this ad-hoc committee. Other members were Wanda A., Fresno, Jan G., Fresno, Peggy K., San Jose, Joan M., San Francisco, Betsy N. and Earthel N., Rancho Cordova and Lisa B., Anderson. In planning for the first meeting, each member obtained a different 12-step service arm's incorporation documents. These were used as the basis for the NCWSA Bylaws. In April 1982, the committee met for the weekend at Earthel's home to create the bylaws. Following the Steps, Traditions and Concepts was imperative to the area and the committee. All opinions and suggestions were carefully evaluated as the document was created. Much progress was made that first weekend. Subsequent meetings were held during the June and October 1982 conferences.

The draft was presented to the NCWSC during the October 1982 committee meeting. Suggestions were made by the committee and included as appropriate. The final bylaws document was approved by the assembly during the February 1983 Assembly in South San Francisco. Betsy N. filed the incorporation document and Bylaws with the State of Calif. in 1983. The NCWSA received its initial determination as a 501c(3) non-profit corporation on January 15, 1985 and the final ruling on March 21, 1988. The area recommended that the districts and information service centers review their tax status as it related to incorporation. They supported the services by sharing their incorporation experience. Some service arms did incorporate. Others obtained only a resale permit, as their business was not extensive. When the state updated the laws on nonprofit corporations, the assembly appointed a new Bylaws Committee, chaired by Jan G. Committee members who served were Art B., San Jose, Peggy C., Los Gatos and LaVonne O., Dublin. In July 1988, a special assembly reviewed the draft of the Bylaws. The committee incorporated many of their recommendations and presented the final document at the annual assembly in September 1988. It was approved with minor changes and was filed with the State of California. During mid 1990's, Becky H. from Berkeley, Bylaws Coordinator, and her committee of Ari T.-F. from San Francisco, Dav G. from Roseville, LaVonne O. from Dublin and Marilyn R. from San Leandro updated the Bylaws. Job descriptions of the coordinators were removed from the bylaws. Instead they were added to the Northern California Committee Guidelines. The major changes were presented and approved by the assembly in 1996. The remaining changes were presented and approved by the assembly in 1997.

Conventions

Independent Alcoholics Anonymous conferences, conventions and round-ups were supported by the Al-Anon fellowship. They include the Serenity in Yosemite, the Monterey Round-Up, the Lake Tahoe Fall Festival, the Spring Fling in Sacramento, Living Sober in San Francisco, Young People's AA Conference and the Growing Together Weekend at Westminster Woods. In most of these gatherings, Al-Anon members are part of the planning committee, and plan the Al-Anon part of the conference.

In 1986, the northern and southern areas of California decided to hold a common convention that was eventually called the California Statewide Convention. The idea of this convention was to unite the two areas in a way that hadn't been done since the division in 1964. The leaders felt that more members from both areas would attend if the convention alternated between Fresno and Bakersfield, since both communities were near the area borders. Three were held, in Fresno (1986), then Bakersfield (1989) and again in Fresno (1992). When it came time to decide on the fourth convention, the CA (SO) area realized that they were hosting the Al-Anon portion of the AA International Convention in San Diego in 1995. They felt they could not ask their members to plan for this convention as well. They suggested that it be held in 1994 and the north countered with a suggestion of 1996. After no agreement could be reached, this convention was dropped from the schedule.

Anonymity in Minutes, Reports and Publications

Unless there is some reason to include last names, such as updating a roster for mailing or providing the delegate's address at conference, only a first name and initial appear in the minutes. The secretary refers to the person by the title of the service they provide as much as possible. The committee roster includes full names and addresses and is given to the committee members, not to the groups. Since 1982, the area newsletter, the *12 Stepper*,[21] usually printed the full names[22] of the committee members and their alternates. The list is important to our groups as resources when they need help. Because a district representative was stalked by an Al-Anon member in the early 1990's, a motion passed that individuals may request that their address and phone number not be published or that pseudonyms or other anonymous methods may be used in place of a last name and an address. One area secretary reported, "One of the trends I noticed was that ideas often took several years for acceptance, and that, much as we try not to, personalities often affect how we accept an idea. Objectivity is served by anonymity. I used the style of reporting that listed the points made without listing the names of the person making the point, usually with bullets. That allowed anyone reading the minutes to look at the idea expressed without attaching a personality to it." One of the projects the secretary took on was to sort the 'motions passed & failed' into chronological order and indexing them so that updates could be done more easily and use less paper. This involved looking back through years of minutes going back to 1967, the earliest year for which minutes were available in the archives.

The Area Committee

The actions of the area committee are listed throughout this book. The purpose of the area committee is defined as follows:

1. To foster communication between districts on common issues. This is done when the district representatives meet at committee meetings, and when the delegate and the coordinators visit district meetings.
2. To disseminate information from the World Service Office to the districts. This is done when the delegate and the coordinator give reports.
3. To do business authorized by the assembly between assemblies. We learn what the officers and committees are doing as they report their actions at the committee meeting and in the *12 Stepper*.
4. To report issues to the assembly through recommendations and motions, and
5. To report unresolved area issues to the World Service Conference through the delegate. Unresolved issues are often found through the process of "Ask-It-Basket" questions. These questions are usually posed during the assembly and often answered by a long-time member. Those questions that are not answered are then discussed at area committee meetings. The delegate has the option of taking any question to the World Service Conference, whether an answer was given or not.

Policy is not created at the area committee level. The assembly creates policy for the area and the World Service Conference creates US and Canada policy. The area committee is responsible for implementing those policies as they affect the area. They may also give direction (for example, how to implement Alateen Sponsor Guidelines), but not enforce any policy or otherwise interfere with the operation of districts, Literature Distribution Centers and Al-Anon Information Services.

Group "delegates" (now called group representatives) attended the first area committee meeting in December 1952 in Santa Rosa. They stated that their purpose was to plan the next conferences and do any other Al-Anon business as necessary. In 1963 the first official assembly of Northern California was formed when the World Service Conference allowed California to divide into North and South. They first met the following winter. District "committeemen" (now called district representatives) met at the same time as this other Conference committee at the AA conference. Both the assembly and the conference planning committee met at the conferences until the Council merged with the assembly in 1970. During the period from 1970 to 1978, assemblies were regularly held three times per year at these AA conferences. After 1978, the area cooperated in holding three conferences with NCCAA each year and the area committee met at those conferences, usually on Saturday morning and later on, all day Saturday. As the needs for business became greater, the committee also met a fourth time away from the conferences. In 1993, the committee decided to meet separately from the NCCAA conferences. The committee meeting began on Friday evening with the district representatives, officers and coordinators meeting separately, followed by a combined meeting all day Saturday. Meetings were held in each section in turn. In that way, the distance traveled equalized for the participants. In the fall of 2000, the committee asked the hosting section to hold a service day at the same location. This experiment was an attempt to encourage more individuals into service.

Executive Committee

In 1987, the Bylaws committee recommended the establishment of a board of directors, because the changes to the non-profit corporation laws required one. The assembly and many Al-Anon members objected to the word "director", since they believed that no one in Al-Anon should "manage and direct." The term Executive Committee (EC) was selected, since this committee is usually part of a board's functions. The term of office was originally one year. After the Bylaws Committee determined the term to be too short to be effective, the term was changed to 18 months in 1994, one-half of a three-year term. Originally, anyone who was a current or a past district representative, including current and past officers, could be elected to the EC. Eventually this was changed to exclude current officers, since the groups believed a conflict of interest could occur. To achieve greater involvement by the groups and to minimize the possibility that the EC members were concentrated geographically, the area divided itself into three sections, North, Central and South. Each section contained full districts and the number of districts chosen for each was based on achieving an equal number of groups in each section. One member was selected from among each of the three sections. The remaining two members were "at-large" members. The section candidates were selected from among the current district representatives by the district representatives in their section. The portion of the Northern California World Service Committee members elected by the group representatives selected the two at large candidates. The Executive Committee (EC) elected its own chairperson and secretary.

Conflict Resolution Guideline

The primary functions of the EC were to assure that the prevailing state and federal laws were being followed, to review the performance of the officers and to report their actions to the assembly.

Reviewing the performance of the officers became very stressful in 1995. The assembly chairperson, after receiving complaints from other committee members, removed the Corresponding Secretary from her position. When the secretary objected, the Executive Committee approved the decision of the chairperson. Some members of the area committee, however, believed that the chairperson didn't have the authority to remove her and requested that a special assembly of the groups be called to decide this. After the May area committee meeting, the chairperson called a special assembly in July 1996. The group representatives voted that the Corresponding Secretary should remain in office.

At the February 1996 area committee meeting, the chairperson appointed a committee to establish a guideline to help in resolving conflicts. This guideline established the principle that parties who are having difficulty in agreeing first speak to each other using the principle of "talk to each other, reason things out etc." Should this not resolve the issue, they may ask someone else in Al-Anon to help them in a mediation mode. Once this is done, they also let another committee member know of the conflict, and include the Executive Committee in any letters and notes they might send each other. The resolution may go from the coordinator to the officer to the Executive Committee and finally to the assembly. In the next term, 1997 to 1999, there were four conflicts that were resolved more or less successfully with this procedure.

Delegate and Trustee assignments

The World Service Office assigns each delegate to a delegate committee. The practice began when the World Service Conference was made permanent in 1964. Southwest Regional trustees are elected from among candidates in the Southwest Region. At-large trustees are elected by the WSO Board of Trustees from anywhere in the US and Canada. Both serve for a three-year term. They may serve a maximum two terms. Trustees are assigned to chair committees. The list shows the delegate and trustee assignment for Al-Anon members from Northern California.

Term	Delegate	WSO Committee
2000-	Marilyn R.	Public Outreach
1997-1999	Cathy C.	Group Services
1994-1996	Art B.	Literature
1991-1993	Peggy C.	Public Information
1988-1990	Mary A.-T.	Alateen
1985-1987	Barbara L.	Conference Committee on Trustees
1982-1984	Jean McL.	Literature
1979-1981	Faun L.	Handbook
1976-1978	Irma C.	Public Information
1973-1975	Bonnie H.	Public Information
1970-1972	Judy W.	Floater (Wasn't assigned to any committee)
1967-1969	Muriel B.	Alateen
1964-1966	Ann O.	Public Relations
1961-1963	Helen B.-R.	No Committees had delegates

Term	Trustee	Type	Committee Chair
1982-1984	Irma C.	Regional	Handbook
1994-1996	Mary A.-T.	Regional	Admissions-Handbook
1997-1999	Mary A.-T.	At Large	Admissions–Handbook

Closing Thoughts

The history of Al-Anon in Northern California is not complete. This book is not complete. We have witnessed in the lifetimes of those who are 50 or older a complete transition from belief that alcoholics were condemned to a lifetime of drinking, insanity and death, to a new belief that with proper treatment the alcoholic can reliably become and remain sober. More importantly for the wives, children, parents and siblings of alcoholics, we have learned that our early approach of condemnation didn't work. We have learned that when we approached the family disease of alcoholism as part of our own problem and used steps similar to that of the alcoholic, we could also restore ourselves to sanity. This *Journey To Recovery* is a chronicle that shows how we organized to find and help those families that continue to struggle with living with an alcoholic. Many of us decided that with the help of a power greater than ourselves we could and did find a better way of life. We can learn from the past and in doing so, we protect the future of Al-Anon and Alateen for our families, friends and relatives who haven't yet joined the Al-Anon way.

Notes

[1] *Al-Anon Faces Alcoholism*, B-1, was first introduced in 1965 and served for many years as the basis of describing the Al-Anon program to the public and to professionals.

[2] *The One Day At a Time in Al-Anon*, B-6, was first introduced in 1968. More than five million copies have been sold.

[3] The original service handbook was one of four pamphlets. Today it is published as *Al-Anon Alateen Service Manual 1998-2000*, P24/27 by Al-Anon Family Group Headquarters, Inc.

[4] *How to Know an Alcoholic* was a pamphlet sold by AFG Headquarters, but produced by the National Council on Alcoholism. It was discontinued in 1976.

[5] *Alcoholism, a Merry-Go-Round Named Denial*, P-3 was adapted by AFG Headquarters, Inc. for Al-Anon use from an article written by Dr. Kellerman.

[6] The Pacific Regional AA Service Assembly (PRAASA) is held with Al-Anon participation on the first weekend in March. The PRAASA region is geographically different from that of Al-Anon's Southwest region.

[7] *Pebbles in the Pond* was discontinued in 1998 and replaced with *The Best of Public Outreach* (P-90).

[8] Motion passed at the March 1978 Assembly.

[9] Regional Service Seminars are conferences sponsored by the WSO in the nine Al-Anon regions to foster a closer connection between the WSO personnel and local and area trusted servants.

[10] The SWRDM is a regional meeting of current and past delegates that prepares new delegates for the World Service Conference.

[11] *Paths to Recovery*, B-24, is published by AFG Headquarters, Inc.

[12] *Having Had a Spiritual Awakening*, B-25, is published by AFG Headquarters, Inc.

[13] *Alcoholism, The Family Disease*, P-4, is published by AFG Headquarters, Inc.

[14] *Alateen Talks Back on Detachment*, P-73, is published by AFG Headquarters, Inc.

[15] *A Guide to Alateen Sponsorship-An Unforgettable Adventure*, P-86, is published by AFG Headquarters, Inc.

[16] *The Dilemma of an Alcoholic Marriage*, B-4, is published by AFG Headquarters, Inc.

[17] While the inventory is ongoing, no decision has been made to make any changes to Conference Approved Literature.

[18] *Sexual Intimacy and the Alcoholic Relationship*, P-77, is published by AFG Headquarters, Inc.

[19] This series of days are fully explained in chapter 7, "Other Communities and Cultures."

[20] Chosen Agenda Items were originally called Red Light–Green Light. Those voted to be green were discussed at the floor of the World Service Conference.

[21] The *12 Stepper* has been the official newsletter for the area since 1970.

[22] A vote by the area committee added the names and addresses of committee members and their alternates to the *12 Stepper* in January 1989.

4

The Hispanic Community

The Hispanic communities are considered by the majority in California as a homogenous community united by a common language. In reality, the communities are composed of families from several Central and South American countries, each of whom have different dialects, customs and drinking habits. It took a while for AA and Al-Anon to form and become part of recovery for Hispanics. It began for non-alcoholics in the late 1960's. But they struggled until the spark of recovery became widespread in the early 1980's. Today, the Hispanic Al-Anon members are full partners with the English community. They fully participate in area events at the area conventions and the area world service committee. They also have developed their own network of support through their Intergroup. This Intergroup has become the focus of their social and recovery activities. They reach out to their own community with public service announcements placed on Spanish language radio and TV stations and by speaking at community events. They have also become partners with the English community in reaching out to the Asian and Middle Eastern communities in the East San Francisco Bay area.

Early Spanish Speaking Groups

In 1968, some wives of alcoholics gathered in San Francisco to open a Spanish-speaking Al-Anon group, the "Latino" group. Mary D., who spoke in English, helped and Gloria was the interpreter. It opened on Saturdays in the avenues in the house of Ana A. with only a few members. Shortly after, they moved to 1329 7th Avenue near Judah and met there for 16 years. Because of the Loma Prieta earthquake, the group moved to Capp St. for about three years and later moved to St. Paul's Church until it closed after 32 years. Not long after the "Latino" group opened its doors, a second group, "Geneva" began to meet on Fridays at Vienna

St. They met for 23 years and closed around 1994. Around 1982, another Spanish group opened, meeting on Monday night in St Anthony's church on Cesar Chavez Street (formerly Army St). This group "Amor y Comprencion", is still open to help families of alcoholics. The next group to open in the city, "Unidad", met on Friday nights at the Corpus Christi Church hall at Alemany and Santa Rosa streets.

The group, "Una Dia A La Vez", opened on August 8, 1981 and met on Thursday nights on 8th Lane in a garage in South San Francisco. Later the group moved to the Senior Center on Grand Ave for a couple years. Then they moved to the Sitike Counseling Center for 12 years. Again they moved, this time to the San Bruno Church Hall in San Bruno. They are now at 405 Grand Ave, Suite #204 in South San Francisco.

"Alegria de Vivir" opened in San Bruno in 1981 at the San Bruno Church hall. They closed about 1990. It re-opened in 1998 and has celebrated its second anniversary. Another Hispanic group in the area, "Fuerza Y Esperanza", meets on Tuesday nights in Redwood City. It has been passing the message to the Hispanic community since 1985. "Gratitud" opened its doors in 1989 in Daly City, meeting on Friday nights on Wellington Ave. Later on, they moved to the Alano Club at 7330 Mission St.

In the East Bay, "Nueva Vida" was the first group to open in Oakland in May1980. This group closed for a while, but re-opened in September, 2000. There was also an early group (formed in 1979) that met in St. Bede's church in Hayward. The "Felicidad" group opened in Richmond in 1981, then moved to San Pablo in 1990. Other groups were founded around the same time in Fresno, Hollister, Sacramento, Salinas, San Rafael, Santa Rosa and San Jose.

Other Spanish Speaking Groups

Another group, also named "Alegria de Vivir", opened August 30, 1998 and meets on Mondays at St. Timothy's Church hall in San Mateo. This group started with just a few members and is growing, with sometimes 10 to 12 members. It has grown for lots of years and lately opened a second meeting on Thursday, with about 18 members—sometimes. In 1995, a group of excited teens spoke with the delegate at the Conevenciones Hispana in Fresno about the idea of a Spanish-speaking meeting for young people. They opened the first Adult Child (ACA) group, "Apprendio a Vivir," in San Jose. Unfortunately, as the members married, had children and other responsibilities, they were unable to remain open. This group closed in 2000. In 1998, another Adult Child (ACA) group "Apprendio a Vivir" opened its doors in South San Francisco. One of the newest groups, Louisa and Anna, was formed in 1999 in Palo Alto. Their unusual name comes about because they wish to honor the co-founders of Al-Anon. Now there are over 35 Spanish Al-Anon and Alateen groups in Northern California. One practice within the Hispanic groups is that many of the groups have more than one meeting per week. In San Jose, for example, the five groups hold twelve meetings each week. There are also Alateen, Preteen and Adult Child meetings available.

Participation in Conventions and Conferences

The Hispanic members have participated in the "Convencion Hispana"[1] since 1976. This is an Al-Anon convention that includes AA participation. For the first ten years the convention was held only in Southern California. In 1987, our Northern California Hispanic groups had the opportunity to host the 8th Convencion Hispana in San Francisco with Dolores G. as the convention chair. This was not an easy experience. The members and the newly elected coordinator were afraid because they were not aware of the convention requirements and responsibilities. And there were no guidelines to follow. This committee asked Marilyn R., the area Alternate Public Information Coordinator, to speak. Since then, the convention has alternated between the north and south. The members learned to work with each other and it became easier to cooperate and do all the fundraising activities necessary to succeed at following conventions. Since 1995, the area delegates, including Art B. (Arturo), Cathy C. and Marilyn R., have been asked to present a report to the Convention. The convention also includes a program for English-speaking people. One English-speaking participant shares, "I attended the 1997 Hispanic Convention in San Francisco and chaired an English speaking meeting. One bilingual member said that this was her first English-speaking meeting. While she could speak both languages, she was terrified to attend English-speaking meetings in her own community. This English meeting at the convention did much to reduce her fears about returning home and attending meetings in both languages."

Hispanic members also have participated with the NCWSA Area Conferences and Conventions, providing both with full programs. Virginia T. shares, "Marilyn R. invited the Spanish-speaking members to participate in the Oakland Conference which was held on July 11-13, 1986."[2] Since then, the Spanish programs have been part of the NCWSA conferences. The Hispanic groups also participated in AA conventions.

Spanish Speaking Coordinators

Shortly after the *Al-Anon's Twelve Steps and Twelve Traditions* was published in 1981, some of the local Spanish-speaking members wanted it for themselves in Spanish. Virginia T. and Teresa met with Marilyn R. to propose a project. The two of them carefully translated the chapters, and Marilyn typed them up. Teresa and Virginia took the drafts and returned with improved versions, until the entire book was translated. Several copies were distributed to Spanish-speaking members. This local translation served the community until the book *Los Doce Pasos y las Doce Tradiciones de Al-Anon* was available from the World Service Office in 1988.

In 1987, the NCWSA established the position of Spanish-Speaking Coordinator in order to assist the Hispanic groups and in forming new groups. The first coordinator, Virginia T., from Oakland, was elected by the Hispanic groups themselves at the September Convención Hispana in Fresno. Elena G., from Sacramento, was elected the Alternate at the next conference in Stockton. Virginia T. shares some of the things she did as coordinator.[3] "Since that time, I have translated all of the flyers and public information announcements, organized programs, provided literature and participated in many activities. In order to facilitate the attendance of Al-Anon/Alateen Spanish speaking meetings, I have worked to provide and encourage the simultaneous participation of AA Spanish speaking groups in the various events. Some of the miscellaneous activities that I have been pursuing in conjunction with my office are: helping to proofread books so that they can be printed in Spanish, translating all of the guidelines for the Conferences and recommendations for the assembly; writing all the districts offering them help for Spanish speaking members and their groups; communicating with lone members, getting in touch with members in Southern California and Mexico; lending tapes to groups; registering various groups, etc."

In 1990, the NCWSA expanded the position to include members with languages other than English and renamed the position, Non-English Speaking Coordinator. In 2000, the position has changed its name again, to Diversity Coordinator, in recognition of the efforts done by both English and Spanish Speaking members to assist in forming a Punjabi/Hindi Group.[4]

Spanish Intergroup Office

The first Spanish Intergroup opened in Southern California and for many years it was responsible for all the groups. Due to the distance and especially the growth of the groups in Northern California, another office opened in South San Francisco in March 1994. The first meeting was at the AA "Solo Por Hoy" office in San Francisco. All the group representatives present, except one, voted to establish an Intergroup. A few months later, Intergroup met at the "29 de Mayo" AA office in South San Francisco. They met for three years at San Bruno's church in San Bruno. They then officially opened the office at 405 Grand Avenue, Suite # 204 in South San Francisco. The Intergroup established the position of Liaison to the NCWSA, and elected Esther G. in 1995 for a partial and then a full term. She served for 4 1/2 years. While she was liaison she brought enthusiasm and awareness about the assembly and committee meetings being connected with the Spanish groups and their activities. She was the first bilingual member that made an effort to speak more Spanish so she could translate information into Spanish. Esther also encouraged other members to attend these meetings to support her. Because of her loving way, the Hispanic community got excited about service. The Intergroup is the center for social services and activities in the Hispanic Al-Anon community. Some of our groups also participate in districts. A geographical boundary is not necessary as long as there is a mutual understanding. The Intergroup provides these functions: a telephone list for those looking for Al-Anon and Alateen; an address to help in communications with the WSO, while maintaining anonymity for the individual Al-Anon members; receives questions by mail and phone and directs individuals to the nearest group; publishes and distributes meeting lists; helps in providing speakers for events and workshops; communicates with the Public Information coordinators through the districts where possible; maintains a literature depot concentrating on the use of Spanish literature; meets with group representatives to resolve problems using the Traditions as a guide; and prints and distributes their own monthly newsletter, *La Antorcha*, which began in September 1996.

Diversity Day

In 1998, the NCWSA held its first Diversity Day. The Hispanic groups enthusiastically participated because they wanted to help the next non-English language person. There were Spanish-speaking participants who came from every country in Central and South America. From the speaker's platform, individuals spoke in their own native language, mostly English and Spanish, but there were those who spoke in German, French, Punjabi and Japanese. Ruth S., a Hispanic member, of South San Francisco, expressed what she felt; "Al-Anon gives us the opportunity to share our culture in the Day of Diversity. We all have the same common problem of alcoholism in our families. Even though we speak a different language, and enjoy a different culture, we are all equal. That creates unity. We prove this by having the theme of the NCWSA annual convention in English and Spanish. I was privileged to be a speaker at the Diversity Day in Berkeley in 1998. It was just great to see that our purpose was achieved, even with different races, cultures and even different foods to share with each other. I was so honored to receive a certificate as thanks for my participation. Thanks to Al-Anon!"

The Hispanic community has transitioned from trying to survive alcoholism, to today being a partner with the English in helping the recovery of families of alcoholics.

Notes

[1] The theme and chairperson of each Hispanic Convention is listed at the end of the chapter.

[2] *12 Stepper*, March 1988, p 7. Reprinted with permission of the publisher.

[3] *12 Stepper*, March 1988, p 7 and 8. Reprinted with permission of the publisher

[4] Punjabi is one of the languages spoken in India. The group was formed for the Indian community in Fremont.

Historia de las Convenciones Hispanas

Año	Lema	Sede	Coordinador
1976	Descubrir grandezas de Al-Anon	Los Ángeles	Rosa B.
1979	Esperanza, fortaleza y experiencia	Los Ángeles	Georgina L.
1980	Aceptación es recuperación	Los Ángeles	Beatriz A.
1982	Solo Por Hoy Con la Ayuda de Al-Anon	Anaheim	Rosa R.
1983	Vive y deja vivir	Los Ángeles	Sonia L.
1985	Un oasis en el desierto	Palm Springs	Maria L.
1986	Una llamada de esperanza	San Diego	Ángel M.
1987	Al-Anon mensaje de amor	San Francisco	Dolores G.
1988	Alegría de vivir	Los Ángeles	Lupe M.
1989	Unidos en la esperanza	Sacramento	Elena G.
1990	Al-Anon sin fronteras	Palm Springs	Amanda M.
1991	Al-Anon mantanial de vivir	Orange County	Maria V.
1992	Puente de amor y esperanza	Oakland	Esther G.
1993	La luz que buscaba llega	Los Ángeles	Celia P.
1994	Nacer, crecer y florecer	San José	Julieta D.
1995	Recuperación, Servicio en acción	Fresno	Amparo M.
1996	Tres legados en acción	Orange County	Francisca E.
1997	Al-Anon, Alateen dos ramas de vida	San Francisco	Isabel G.
1998	Abriendo puertas de crecimiento y armonía	Los Ángeles	Salvador J.
1999	Compartiendo los tesoros de Al-Anon y Alateen	Santa Clara	Lupe N.
2000	Fortaleza, esperanza y amor	Whittier	Guadalupe R.

5

La Comunidad Hispana

Las comunidades hispanas son consideradas, por la mayoría de la gente de California, como una comunidad enorme unida por un lenguaje común. En realidad, las comunidades están compuestas de familias de varios países de Centro y Sur América. Cada país tiene sus diferentes dialectos, costumbres y hábitos de beber. Al igual las familias hispanohablantes se sienten aislados de la cultura predominante por su propio lenguaje. Tardó bastante para que A.A. y Al-Anon se formaran y fueran parte de la recuperación para los hispanos. Al-Anon comenzó para los no-alcohólicos los últimos años de los '60. Batallaron muchísimo hasta lograr dispersar una chispa de recuperación por muchas partes en los primeros años de los '80. Ahora, la comunidad hispana de Al-Anon es compañera participe con la comunidad de habla inglesa. Participando totalmente en los eventos de área a nivel de las convenciones y con el comité de área del servicio mundial. También han desarrollado su propia cadena de apoyo por medio de su oficina intergrupal. Esta oficina intergrupal ha sido el enfoque de sus actividades sociales y de recuperación. Extiende el mensaje a sus propias comunidades por medio de los anuncios de servicio público en las estaciones de radio y TV, y también hablando en sus eventos comunitarios. Se ha asociado también con la comunidad de habla inglesa, extendiendo la ayuda para la gente asiática y del Medio Oriente que vive en las ciudades del este de la Bahía de San Francisco.

Los primeros grupos de habla hispana

En 1968, algunas esposas de alcohólicos se juntaron en la ciudad de San Francisco para abrir un grupo de Al-Anon en español, el grupo "Latino". Mary D., que hablaba inglés, les ayudó, y Gloria fue su intérprete. Se reunía el grupo los sábados, en la casa de Ana A. en las avenidas, con muy pocos miembros. Poco después, se movió a la 7ma Avenida, no. 1329, cerca de Judah, y sesionó allí por 16 años. Se movió a la calle Capp por unos tres años, después del terremoto de la Loma Prieta (1989), y después sesionó en la iglesia de San Pablo, hasta que cerró después de 32 años. Poco después de que el grupo "Latino" abrió sus puertas, un segundo grupo, "Geneva", empezó a reunirse los viernes en la calle Viena. Estuvieron sus puertas abiertas como por 23 años, hasta cerrarse en 1994. Como en 1982, un tercer grupo hispano abrió sus puertas, reuniéndose los lunes por la noche en la iglesia de San Antonio en la calle Cesar Chávez (anteriormente Army St.). Este grupo, "Amor y Comprensión", todavía sigue ayudando a los familiares de alcohólicos. El siguiente grupo que se abrió en la ciudad, "Unidad", sesionaba los viernes por la noche, en el salón de la iglesia Hábeas Cristi, por las calles Alemany y Santa Rosa. El grupo "Un Día a la Vez" se abrió el 8 de agosto de 1981 y sesionaba los jueves por la calle 8va (Lane), en Sur San Francisco, en un garaje. Después se movió al Centro de Ancianos por la Avenida Grand, por dos años. Y luego se movió al Centro de Consejería Sitike, donde se quedó unos 12 años. Otra vez se movió el grupo, esta vez fuera de la ciudad a la iglesia de San Bruno, en San Bruno. Ahora sesiona en el 405 de la Avenida Grand, sala #204, en Sur San Francisco. "Alegría de Vivir" se abrió en San Bruno en 1981, en el salón de la iglesia de San Bruno, cerrándose en 1990. En 1998 se volvió a abrir y este año, 2000, celebró su segundo aniversario El grupo "Gratitud" se abrió en 1989 en Daly City, reuniéndose los viernes por la Avenida Wellington. Después se movió al Club Alano en la calle Misión, no. 7330. El primer grupo que se abrió en Oakland fue "Nueva Vida", en mayo de 1980. Este grupo se cerró por un tiempo, pero se volvió a abrir el 16 de Septiembre del 2000. Había también otro grupo temprano (que se formó en 1979) que se reunía en la iglesia de St. Bedes, en Hayward. El grupo "Felicidad" se abrió en Richmond en 1981, y se movió a San Pablo en 1990. Otros grupos se iniciaron por esta misma época en Fresno, Hollister, Sacramento, Salinas, San Rafael, Santa Rosa y San José.

Otros grupos de habla hispana

Otro grupo, también llamado "Alegría de Vivir", comenzó al fin de agosto de 1998 y se reunió los lunes en la iglesia de San Timoteo, en San Mateo. Este grupo abrió con muy poca gente y sigue aumentándose hasta tener 10 o 12 miembros. Otro grupo hispano en la área, "Fuerza y Esperanza", se ha reunido los martes desde 1985, en el Centro de la Comunidad de Redwood City, y sigue pasando el mensaje a la comunidad hispana. Ha crecido tanto a través de los años que recientemente abrió una segunda reunión, los jueves, que a veces atrae unos 18 miembros. Uno de los grupos más recién formados, "Luisa y Ana", se formó en 1999 en Palo Alto. Su nombre único se debe a que el grupo quería honrar a las dos fundadoras de Al-Anon (Lois y Ann). Hoy día existen más de 30 grupos hispanohablantes en el norte de California.[1] Es muy común entre los grupos hispanos tener más de una sesión por semana. Por ejemplo, en San José, los cinco grupos dan doce sesiones cada semana. Además se encuentran reuniones de Alateen, Preteen y los Hijos Adultos de alcohólicos.

Participación en Convenciones y Conferencias

Los miembros hispanos han participado en las "Convenciones Hispanas" desde 1976. Esta convención de Al-Anon incluye la participación de A.A. Por los primeros diez años las convenciones se llevaron a cabo solamente en el sur de California, hasta que, en 1987, los grupos hispanos del norte de California tuvieron la oportunidad de llevar acabo la 8va Convención Hispana en San Francisco, Dolores G. siendo la Coordinadora. Esta no fue una experiencia fácil. Los miembros nuevamente elegidos a ser Coordinador tenían miedo, por que no sabían los requisitos y responsabilidades de una convención. Y en ese entonces no había guías a seguir. Este comité le invitó a Marilyn R., la Coordinadora Alterna de Información Publica de la área, que compartiera. Desde entonces, la convención alterna entre el norte y el sur. Los miembros aprendieron a trabajar en equipo y a cooperar unos con otros en actividades para recaudar los fondos necesarios para tener éxito en las próximas convenciones. Desde 1995, se les ha pedido a los delegados de la área, incluyendo a Art B. (Arturo), Cathy C., y Marilyn R., dar un reporte a la Convención. La convención también incluye un programa para la gente de habla inglesa. Un miembro que hablaba puro inglés, compartió su participación, diciendo: "Yo asistí a la Convención Hispana en 1997 en San Francisco y coordiné una junta de inglés. Un miembro bilingüe dijo que esta había sido su primera junta en inglés. Pudiendo hablar los dos idiomas, se sentía aterrorizada al asistir una junta en ingles en su propia comunidad. Esta junta en inglés en esta Convención le ayudó mucho a superar sus miedos para poder regresar a casa y acudir a las juntas en los dos idiomas."

Varios miembros hispanos también han participado con las conferencias regionales (NCWSA) y las convenciones, proveyendo programas completos en los dos idiomas.[2] Virginia T. comparte, "Marilyn R. invitó a los miembros de habla hispana a participar en la Conferencia de Oakland que se llevó a cabo el 11-13 de julio de 1986." Desde entonces los programas de temas en español, han sido parte de las Conferencias y Convenciones de NCWSA. Los grupos hispanos también han participado en las Convenciones Hispanas de A.A.

Coordinadoras de habla hispana

Poco después de que *Los Doce Pasos y las Doce Tradiciones de Al-Anon* fuera publicado en 1981, algunos de los miembros locales de habla hispana, lo querían para ellos mismos en español. Virginia T. Y Teresa se juntaron con Marilyn R. para proponer un proyecto. Las dos cuidadosamente tradujeron los capítulos, y Marilyn los escribió a maquina. Teresa y Virginia agarraron las primeras versiones del borrador, lo mejoraron y se lo regresaron a Marilyn hasta completar las traducciones completas de todo el libro. Varias copias del borrador fueron distribuidas a los miembros de habla hispana. Esta traducción local sirvió a la comunidad hasta que el libro *Los Doce Pasos y las Doce Tradiciones de Al-Anon* estuvo disponible en las oficinas del Servicio Mundial en 1988.

En 1987, la NCWSA estableció la posición de Coordinadora de Habla Hispana para poder ayudar a los grupos hispanos a formar grupos nuevos. La primera Coordinadora Virginia T., de Oakland, fue elegida por los mismos grupos hispanos en la Convención de septiembre, en Fresno. Elena G., de Sacramento, fue elegida como Alterna en la Conferencia NCWSA de Stockton. Virginia T. comparte algunas de las cosas que hizo como Coordinadora: "Yo traduje los volantes y anuncios públicos para esta conferencia. También estuve en contacto con los medios de comunicación y organicé el programa de temas en español, proveyendo literatura y participando en muchas actividades. Para poder facilitar la asistencia en las juntas en español de Al-Anon/Alateen, he trabajado para proveer y alentar la participación simultánea en varios eventos de los grupos de habla hispana de A.A. Algunas de las actividades misceláneas que he seguido en conjunto con mi servicio son: ayudar a revisar los libros que se imprimen en español; traducir todas las guías para las Conferencias y recomendaciones a la Asamblea; escribir a todos los distritos ofreciéndoles ayuda con sus miembros y sus grupos; comunicarme con los miembros solitarios; estar en contacto con miembros en el sur de California y en México; prestárles cintas (*cassettes*) a los grupos; registrar grupos, etc." En 1990, la NCWSA extendió la posición para incluir a miembros que hablan otros lenguajes, que no fueran de habla inglesa, y la llamaron Coordinadora "Non-English". En el 2000 el título de la posición se cambió otra vez, a Coordinadora de Diversidad, en reconocimiento de los esfuerzos hechos por los miembros de habla inglesa e hispana para ayudar a formar un grupo Punjabi/Hindi.[3]

Oficina Intergrupal Hispana

La primera Oficina Intergrupal[4] Hispana se abrió en el sur de California y por muchos años fue responsable por todos los grupos hispanos. Por la distancia y especialmente por el crecimiento de los grupos en el norte de California, otra oficina Intergrupal se abrió en Sur San Francisco en marzo de 1994. Todos los representantes de grupos presente, excepto uno, votaron para establecer esta oficina. De allí la primera junta se llevó a cabo en la oficina del grupo "Sólo Por Hoy" de A.A. en San Francisco. Algunos meses después, se reunió en la oficina del grupo "29 de Mayo" de Sur San Francisco. Se reunió en la iglesia de San Bruno por tres años y por fin se abrió oficialmente la oficina, que está localizada en el 405 de la Avenida Grand, sala #204, en Sur San Francisco. La oficina Intergrupal estableció la posición de Enlace a la NCWSA, por primera vez y se eligió a Esther G., en 1995 por un período parcial y después por otro periodo completo. Ella dio su servicio por cuatro años y medio. Como Enlace, ella trajo entusiasmo y conocimiento sobre las juntas de la Asamblea y del Comité del Área, conectándolos con los grupos hispanos y sus actividades. Fue el primer miembro bilingüe que hizo todo el esfuerzo por aprender a hablar más español y traducir la información en español. Esther también motivó y retó a otros miembros a acompañarla a estas juntas, pidiendo su apoyo. Por su manera amorosa y fraternal, la comunidad hispana se entusiasmó en el servicio. Esta oficina Intergrupal es el centro de los servicios sociales, además de las actividades, de la comunidad hispana de Al-Anon. Algunos grupos hispanos participan al nivel de sus distritos y se ve que no importan las barreras geográficas porque tenemos una comprensión mutua. La "Intergrupal" ofrece varios servicios: una lista telefónica para aquellos que buscan Al-Anon y Alateen; domicilios para ayudar en la comunicación con la Oficina de Servicios Mundial; mantiene el anonimato individual de los miembros de Al-Anon; recibe preguntas por correo; dirige a personas a los grupos más cercanos; publica y distribuye un directorio de los grupos; ayuda a invitar a los oradores para los eventos y talleres; se comunica con las coordinadoras de información pública en los distritos cuando es posible; mantiene su propio centro de literatura en español, facilitando así su venta y pedidos rápidos; se reúne con los representantes de grupos para resolver problemas, usando las Doce Tradiciones como guía; imprime y distribuye su propio boletín, *La Antorcha*, que comenzó en septiembre de 1996.

Un día de diversidad

En 1998, la NCWSA, tuvo su primer Día de Diversidad. Los grupos hispanos entusiástas participaron porque querían ayudar a la próxima persona que no hablara inglés. Hubo participantes de habla hispana cuyas raíces eran de casi todos los países de Centro y Sur América. En la plataforma de Oradores, los individuos compartieron en su propio lenguaje nativo, la mayoría inglés y español, pero hubo algunos que compartieron en alemán, francés, punjabi y japonés. Ruth S., un miembro hispano, de Sur San Francisco, expresa lo que sintió, "Al-Anon nos da la oportunidad de compartir culturas en este día de Diversidad. Todos tenemos el mismo problema común de alcoholismo en nuestras familias. Aunque hablemos diferentes idiomas y disfrutamos una cultura diferente, todos somos iguales. Eso crea unidad. Comprobamos esto poniendo el tema de la Convención Anual de NCWSA en inglés y español. Y tuve el privilegio de ser una de las oradoras para el Día de Diversidad en Hayward en 1998. Fue grandioso ver que nuestro propósito se había logrado, aun con diferentes razas, culturas ... hasta las comidas, compartimos unos con otros. Para mí fue un gran honor recibir un certificado de agradecimiento por mi participación. Gracias a Al-Anon!"

La comunidad hispana ha logrado progresar, desde sus primeros esfuerzos para sobrevivir con el alcoholismo, hasta llegar hoy, a ser una comunidad hispana, compañera participe con la comunidad de habla inglesa de Al-Anon en la recuperación de las familias de los alcohólicos.

Notes

[1] La lista completa de los grupos hispanohablantes está en el Apéndice.

[2] El tema y la coordinadora de cada Convención Hispana se encuentra en el Apéndice.

[3] Punjabi es uno de los lenguajes que se habla en la India. Se formó el grupó para la comunidad india de Fremont.

[4] La Intergrupal sirve para conectar a los varios grupos locales, ofreciéndoles servicios centralizados. Puede coordinar las actividades, la literatura, y los eventos de varios grupos, además de alentar los nexos entre miembros de los diferentes grupos.

6

Alateen

Early Involvement of Children of Alcoholics

Bob S.[1] recently shared from a podium that he is the only person living who was present when his father, Dr. Bob met Bill W. in Akron on Mother's Day 1935. His sister Sue had already left their home, though she returned from time to time. Seventeen at the time, he had no real interest in the activities of his parents. He relates, "For most of my life, AA didn't have any personal meaning. I never told anyone my Dad was instrumental in starting AA."[2] He jokes now about how he is the oldest living Alateen[3]. Lois had several miscarriages and didn't bear any children. Bill and Lois W.'s attempts to adopt a child proved a failure because of his drinking.

A letter written by the General Secretary[4] of AFG Headquarters dated May 10, 1954 says in part, "We have been trying to find out from the Alcoholic Foundation[5] and the National Committee on Alcoholism[6] if there is any material available on the subject of children of AA's without success. Apparently this is a topic upon which very little has been written, but one that is very important. We know that in June, the Northern California Council is planning a separate session for the teenagers of AA's."[7]

Northern California's Earliest Al-Anon Efforts for Teens

In 1956, an Oakland mother wrote to AFG Headquarters in New York and asked, in reference to a teenaged friend, "How old must an alcoholic relative be to attend

Themes of the NoCAC Conferences

Year	Theme	Logo
1979	We've Only Just Begun	Tree with Sunset and Water below tree
1980	We came to Believe, 2nd time around	Various Animals headed to NOCAC 80
1981	Together we can make it	Little kids going down the road to NOCAC
1982	Life is a song let's sing it together	World with music notes around it
1983	Stairway to Serenity	Books labeled Service, Unity, Recovery, Sunset
1984	Sharing More in 84	Guy & Girl walking on beach
1985	Sharing our Love	Guy & Girl Hugging
1986	When you need a Friend...	Alateen Logo
1987	Growing with the Feelings	Hand holding gloved hand
1988	New beginnings A magnificent reality	Tree Similar to tree for 1979
1989	Making a Difference Together	Square Box with 89 NOCAC
1990	Sailing toward Serenity, The Journey of the Decade	Sailboat with Sail being the logo
1991	Finding the Courage to Grow	Two Lions on logo
1992	Strength Serenity	Green Turtle
1993	Lean on me NoCAC 1993	Guy leaning on NoCAC
1994	Serenity 1994	Flower
1995	Universal Unity	Face and Moon
1996	Spiritual Awakenings	Triangles with faces in them
1997	Step by Step	Foot with Step by Step on it
1998	Progress not Perfection— followed by all 20 Themes	Pattern similar to Alateen book
1999	A Day At A Time in 99	
2000	Eleven More to Go	Baby stepping up to a ladder

Al-Anon meetings?" The answer she received, "There is no age limit set for membership" in Al-Anon.

In April 1957, a member of the Sacramento Nalano Group asked for help from the World Service Office in starting an Al-Anon group for teenagers. Lois W. was already in contact with Bill M., an AA member and prime mover in the establishment of Alateen in Pasadena, CA. The reply from the office included a list of three existing Alateen meetings: two in Southern California and one in South Africa. In a letter to another group, Lois said, "I have always loved the children of AA members. In the early days young teenagers often attended the meetings with other members of the family. The AA program fulfilled the idealism of youth. It not only helped children to understand their alcoholic parents, but also enabled them to apply the principles to themselves, although not always consciously."[8]

In the fall of 1957, the World Service Office sent the Sacramento Nalano Group the new Alateen Traditions that the Pasadena Group had written and the August 1957 *AA Grapevine* article *It's a Teenaged Affair.*[9] Shortly after a copy of the *Grapevine*[10] article appeared, several Northern California groups asked how to start Alateen groups. These included the San Jose Group, the Eureka group and the North Highlands (Greater Sacramento) group.[11]

At the Fall 1961 Northern California Council Conference, held in Pacheco, there were 900 AA and Al-Anon members in attendance. Four teens spoke. One of the speakers, a 17-year-old Oakland Alateen member with 2 1/2 years in Alateen, represented the Hayward group. This teen also mentioned that the seven Bay Area Alateen groups formed an Alateen Intergroup office in San Francisco. These Alateen groups also made an offer to the Al-Anon Clearing House[12] to write a book for Alateens. The Clearing House gently suggested that writing a book or pamphlet was a large undertaking, and that the groups could assist the WSO in developing its own first Alateen book.

In 1963, the Northern California Al-Anon Council invited an Alateen group representative from the San Jose Alateen Group to be a member. The WSO also asked this group for input to the Alateen portion of the 1965 AA International Convention held in Toronto. The World Service Office surveyed Alateen groups throughout the 1960's. At least 21 Northern California Alateen groups responded. In 1967, the Modesto group reported that the age range for their group was 9 to 13 years. This appears to be the earliest record of a preteen Alateen group in Northern California.

The earliest problem listed in the NCWSA records came from an 18-year-old Alateen member from Napa who said, "We do not have an Alateen group any more because a Mr. S. 'would not leave us alone'."

Northern California Alateen Conference (NoCAC)

Long before NoCAC was formed, teens were part of the Al-Anon and AA conferences. An Alateen workshop at the February 1966 Northern California Conference discussed the topic, "Talking in the Meeting" with 35 in attendance. The two-page report gives many suggestions about that topic. Alateens formed an annual conference in 1971, but it was discontinued in 1974. During the summer of 1978, two Alateens, Tim H. and Randy T.[13] from Northern California attended the Southern California Alateen Conference (SCAC). They returned inspired and excited to start a new conference, NoCAC. A committee of teens adapted the SCAC guidelines to fit Northern California circumstances. Since the SCAC was held in the summer at a college, the NOCAC Alateens decided to hold their conference in a hotel in November. This provided both dorm and hotel experiences to those who attended both conferences. At the February 1979 assembly, the teens approached the NCWSA Assembly for start-up funds. Because the plans were vague, the assembly didn't provide any funds. Many members contributed to the NoCAC fund on an individual basis and others provided support by attending their fundraising activities. Thanks to the efforts of Tim H., who was elected the first chairperson, Pat F., from Alameda, the co-chair, Gary B., Pleas S. and Randy T., committee members, NoCAC began again in November 1979 at the Lemington Hotel in Oakland with 102 members in attendance. Almost half the Alateens came from Southern California, as they wholeheartedly supported the efforts to begin NoCAC. At the 10th annual Conference in 1988, there were 483 teens and sponsors present.

In 1983, the Northern California World Service Committee invited the NoCAC Chairperson to be an official member of the area committee. That same year, the area assembly voted to provide a small grant of $300.00 to NoCAC. In 1986, the assembly accepted legal responsibility for NoCAC convention. This gave the teens a way to use the non-profit status of NCWSA, use of the non-profit postage discounts, and liability insurance in negotiating with hotels. It also helped to assure Al-Anon members that the Conference would be well managed. NoCAC's finances, though kept separate, are merged with the assembly's finances for purposes of state and federal non-profit reporting requirements.

Surprising to many adults is the welcome the teens receive from the hotels. They often find themselves negotiating with several hotels in the Holiday Inn and Hilton chains. They have been encouraged to return to those they stayed at in earlier years. The teens develop their own theme[14] and agenda each year.

Today's NoCAC Committee is composed of 12 to 14 teens and two sponsors. They use well-developed guidelines that describe how the committee and the sponsors are selected and who is eligible to serve. They have several fundraisers and fun events, including two potluck speaker meetings that include a dance, and two bashes (campouts) during the year. The NCWSA grant is now $1,000. The Alateens also have a scholarship fund to assist those teens who are unable to afford the full expenses of the registration cost. For the past few years, attendance has ranged from 250 to 350 total. Attendance is restricted to those Alateen members who are at least 12 years old, their sponsors and Al-Anon members interested in becoming sponsors. Attendance still includes some Alateens from Southern California, Nevada, Oregon, Washington, Arizona and sometimes Canada. About one-third of those attending are adults. Adults who become involved are always amazed that the teens themselves successfully present an intense, educational and fun conference, raising and handling $40,000 or more each year.

Preteen Alateen Groups

Meetings for preteens, some as young as six, but most with a minimum age of 8 were formed in the 1960's. They were called by various names, such as, Preteen, Alatot, Ala-Child and Alakid. In the 1990's the name for most preteen groups settled down to Preteen Alateen. As mentioned earlier, the earliest known group for children under the age of 13 existed in Modesto in 1967. Another early preteen group from Boulder Creek began a newsletter called *The Alatot Trailblazer*. The October 1968 Issue survives in Northern California archives. "The purpose of this fellowship is to teach children the nature of alcoholism and how to grow up creatively in an environment where alcoholism is or has been present." Many preteen groups formed during the 1980's, including groups in Hayward, Livermore, Sacramento, San Francisco, San Jose and Santa Rosa. One member shares, "There was no practical information available in 1980 about how to conduct a meeting for preteens." The WSO replied to his letter with the caution that meetings for younger members could lead to teaching, which was in conflict with the Al-Anon philosophy. He continues, "With this knowledge, the sponsors asked a teacher to become one of the sponsors, so she could assure the sponsors that they weren't teaching. It became obvious to us over the years that children were profoundly affected by alcoholism and they knew it. We couldn't keep a meeting on track for the entire duration of an adjacent Al-Anon meeting, so activities like drawing feelings, making God-boxes and singing were developed for these youngsters."

Some meetings met at the same time as Al-Anon meetings that were one and one-half hours long. In these cases, the Preteen meeting often had songs and "play time" after the first hour, while other Al-Anon meetings shortened their meeting time to accommodate the preteens. Experience began to show that meetings of one hour were best.

In 1994, the delegate, Art B., shares about his conversation with a group representative of a Hayward Preteen Group. "This ten-year-old girl came up to me and asked what I did as a delegate. I sat down so I could look at her face-to-face and asked her if she knew what her job as group representative included. She explained how she had to come to the assembly to participate, take notes and then report to her group what happened. I explained that my job was similar. I go to a meeting of all delegates from the United States and Canada to participate, and then report to the assembly what I learned. For me it was a revelation that the position of delegate could be described as that of a group representative's representative."

Teen Communications

In 1987, the area teens, with the help of the area Alateen Coordinator and her Alternate, began publishing a newsletter called *Alateen Express*. It usually contains information about upcoming events, the NoCAC registration information, the Alateen Sponsor Guidelines and personal sharings. Since then, two to six issues each year have been sent to the area Alateen groups and the Northern California World Service Committee.

When the Northern California area set up a web site in 1997, an important part of this new medium of communications became the Alateen Page. Included in this section of the web site are a short description of Alateen itself, several pamphlets about Alateen and an invitation for Al-Anon members to become Alateen sponsors. The *Alateen Express* is displayed as part of the Newsletters section.

Limited Access Alateen in Schools, Institutions and Youth Centers

The Al-Anon World Service Office has long encouraged Al-Anon members to sponsor Alateen meetings in high schools. To accomplish this goal took coordination with school officials, students and Alateen sponsors. In most instances only the students in the facility are eligible to attend, which created the term, Limited Access. By the mid-1980's, many Al-Anon districts had meetings in schools. Meeting times varied with each school district; some met before school started, others after the school session ended and some during the lunch period. There were also meetings that rotated throughout the daily schedule so the students wouldn't always miss the same class. In other schools, the Alateen meeting remained constant and the scholastic schedule rotated regularly.

Counselors or nurses referred most students to meetings, but others found the Alateen meeting from announcements on the bulletin board or in the student newsletter. Larger school campuses were able to protect the student's anonymity better than those on small campuses.

Alateen meetings in schools dwindled as special school administration criteria for meetings increased. As the number of school counselors and nurses reduced, principals and deans were increasingly responsible for recommending Alateen to their students. Some schools required the presence of a teacher at the Alateen meeting. Many Alateen sponsors became reluctant to serve as sponsors under these conditions. Teens were also reluctant to speak in front of a teacher. In spite of this, there are a few administrators throughout Northern California who understand our purpose and support the establishment of Alateen meetings.

In the late 1990's, there are few Alateen meetings in the Middle or Elementary schools. Most colleges and universities have Al-Anon and Al-Anon Adult Child meetings available for their students.

Marty H. in District 18 sponsored an Alateen meeting in the Youth Authority Correction Facility in Stockton. Dan P. and Carol sponsored an Alateen meeting in the Belmont Hills Mental Institute for teens in Belmont in District 13. In the early 1990's, there was an Alateen meeting on the Hoopa Indian Reservation about 60 miles from Eureka in District 1.

Beginning in 1985, there has been an Alateen meeting in San Jose's Juvenile Hall. "I received a telephone request from 'Friends Outside'[15] for an Alateen meeting at the juvenile hall facility," Emily P. said. "I called my sponsor, Peggy K., who was one of the pioneers of institutions work in Northern California. She gave me some direction and a list of questions I could ask. Her experience proved to be a great encouraging factor. She helped to lessen my fear of doing the unknown by reminding me that we all have to begin at the beginning.

"Having studied the Al-Anon Institutions Service guidelines, I was prepared for our first meeting with facility personnel. At that meeting I brought another Al-Anon member, knowledge of the Al-Anon/Alateen program, a list of questions, and Conference Approved Literature. We asked questions about the facility, and we gave them information about specific Al-Anon Traditions that address confidentiality, adherence to our principle of anonymity, and the fact that we are all volunteers. They in turn gave us a briefing on rules and regulations of their facility, procedures for clearance, and information on the type of clients[16] housed at the facility. Among the rules are a requirement to keep confidential 'all information regarding the youngsters,' not to give any information that allows the youngsters to contact the sponsor outside the juvenile hall and to report any youngster who is depressed, abused or threatens harm. This may have been an attempt at humor. The regulation says in part, "Some of these children resemble teenagers." We discussed how often we could meet and when. We were taken on a tour of the facility. There was even an emergency phone in case there was trouble during the meeting.

"Those Al-Anon members who were willing to give service at the juvenile hall facility completed a clearance form permitting a background check on individuals going into a 'locked facility.' We were told that this clearance would allow us to enter other facilities as well, such as 'Friends Outside' and later 'The Bill Wilson Center.'[17] We had so many volunteers at one point that we had to put them on a waiting list.

"On our first night, there were five Al-Anon members and two or three new Alateens. We used *Alateen, Hope for Children of Alcoholics* for the meeting's format, as well as *Alateen—A Day at a Time* and other Conference Approved Literature. We originally met two nights a week and were never sure how many teens would be present at either meeting. Each meeting varied in size from two to thirty teens. This particular facility continues to allow Al-Anon to bring Alateen meetings to the teens, which now meets once a week on Thursday.

"We held a regular monthly workshop to allow volunteers to ask questions and to share with one another what they were experiencing. I learned right along with everyone else. We listened as volunteers shared the excitement of overcoming their fears about going inside a locked facility. It was a very exciting period of service to experience. At one of these workshops, the Juvenile Hall Director spoke about the importance of the Alateen meeting. He said that the staff counselors are prevented by law to have any contact with inmates after they leave the facility. He believes that Alateen serves as a bridge to the community and offers them continuing support after they leave."

Alateen Sponsorship

From the inception of Alateen, the use of adult Al-Anon and AA members as sponsors of the Alateen groups was integral to the structure of Alateen. It was an AA member who sponsored the first Alateen group in Pasadena. A 1962 document notes "Board members[18] commented on a problem which is not yet solved; the difficulty of finding Al-Anon members sufficiently interested and grateful to be willing to act as sponsors." In 1965, the World Service Conference approved a *Questionnaire for Sponsors*, which was sent to each proposed group in order to determine the background and qualifications of the sponsors. The responses from groups in Northern California showed that the 21 Alateen groups had a total of 16 Al-Anon and 10 AA sponsors.

In the spring of 1972, the Santa Clara Valley Intergroup (SCVI) gave an Alateen co-sponsor who was also the SCVI Alateen Coordinator $25.00 to start an Alateen Sponsors' Workshop. The Alateen sponsors met monthly to discuss, plan and implement Alateen group activities to attract more teens to the groups. At the beginning of each school year, this committee assembled and distributed packets of literature to junior and senior high schools, community colleges and family support centers. In 1997, they reached 3,150 students at 14 elementary schools, 6 high schools and 2 colleges.

The sponsors formed the AA/I[19] committee and held the first annual "Alcoholism and the Family" Conference in 1974 with 115 persons attending. In 1997, there were workshops and speakers at the conference. In addition, the film *Romance to Recovery* with Joseph A. Pursch MD, was shown.

Helen R., the Northern California Alateen coordinator, proposed the first Alateen Sponsor Guidelines to the assembly in March 1974. In the 1980's in Northern California, concerns were raised about the possibility that persons who harmed children had become Alateen sponsors. This caused the Al-Anon membership to search out solutions to protecting the teens and the Alateen program. In February 1987, the *Practical Applications for Alateen* was presented to the assembly. In February 1988, the Northern California Assembly approved this set of Alateen sponsor guidelines.

The suggestion was that these practical applications be included as part of the Alateen meeting opening. These were provided to the districts as an option for strengthening and protecting the Alateen program in their districts. The guidelines suggest attracting Alateen sponsor candidates through the Alateens themselves, by their current group sponsor and by making regular announcements at district and group business meetings. The guidelines ask the sponsor candidate to answer several questions about their involvement in the disease of alcoholism and the reasons why they would like to serve. The Alateen members also ask that candidates attend several Alateen meetings where they might sponsor prior to being selected by the teens. The Alateen members are encouraged to share their feelings about the candidate and then vote by written ballot to prevent peer pressure from dominating the vote.

Practical Applications for Alateen

1. This is your meeting. You have a say in the structure. Discussion should be encouraged in a group inventory.
2. You can have a group conscience in any matter, including who your sponsor is.
3. You have a right to say NO to any behavior you feel is against the principles of the Program. Any pressure or unfairness can be discussed with other Alateens or Al-Anons.
4. You do not have to be a victim. You do have choices.
5. You can determine what manipulative actions are, and you can stop them.
6. Above all, remember that love is what keeps us together and the 12 Steps lead us to recovery.

It also suggests that Alateen groups occasionally hold an open meeting where Al-Anon members may attend to observe how Alateen works and by including Alateens in speaking at Al-Anon functions and fundraisers. These activities serve to remove the mystique about what goes on in Alateen meetings.

All Alateen meetings in Northern California received copies of these guidelines. They have been the basis of selecting sponsors for several years and continue to be used in 2000.

The current area Alateen Coordinator[20] shares her opinion about Alateen sponsorship today, "Alateen sponsors are a vital part of the Alateen program. Sponsors are there primarily to make sure that meetings are a safe environment for the teens. Alateen sponsors work with the teens, not against them, even though at times this does happen. Alateens need the support and guidance from someone who has more experience in life. Al-Anon sponsors work with the teens in guiding them through the process of learning the principles of the program, offering their experience, strength and hope in the Al-Anon program, and providing stability in the teens lives. Often, teens do not have anyone stable, consistent or supportive in their lives. The Alateen group and the sponsor help to provide that stability.

"I am unsure of how many groups in Northern California use the area guidelines, but we are working on getting the guidelines revised and sent out to the groups and coordinators—since the last revision was in 1988. Alateen sponsors use whatever tools they need to help them, including the pamphlet, *Guide for*

Sponsors of Alateen Groups[21], the book *A Guide to Alateen Sponsorship—an Unforgettable Adventure*, the WSO guidelines, and other literature related to sponsorship. Alateen sponsors also use other sponsors and Al-Anon members as resources as well.

"Alateen has been a part of many teenagers living in Northern California. I can personally attest to this, as I am one who without the program would not be where I am today."

Alateen is Part of the Al-Anon Structure

Part of the teen's responsibilities is in doing 12th Step work and part is in giving back to their community. In 1960, the Alateen Intergroup based in San Francisco wanted to write a book for teens in Alateen recovery. The World Service Office encouraged them to participate in the WSO book, *Alateen, Hope for Children of Alcoholics*[22]. Later on, the San Jose Alateen Group was asked to contribute to the agenda of the 1965 AA International Convention held in Toronto, Canada.

When the Northern California Assembly and the Northern California Council merged in 1970, the assembly established the position of Alateen Coordinator and appointed Estella E., an African-American woman from Woodland, as the first coordinator. In 1977, Irma C., as delegate, appointed Tim H. of San Lorenzo as the first Alateen representative to the NCWSC Committee. The following year, the position of Alateen Liaison was established with a two-year term and the liaison was elected by the Alateens. Today, the Alateen Coordinator is an adult who has been or is an Alateen sponsor, elected by the NCWSC and the Liaison is a teen selected by the coordinator to directly represent teen issues at the NCWSC committee meetings and the assembly.

In the mid 1980's, three ad hoc Alateen Committees developed a series of guidelines called *Alateen Rights*, *Alateen Behavior at Conferences* guidelines and *Alateen Sponsor Guidelines*, which were approved by successive Assemblies.[23] From 1983 to 1988, as many as forty Alateen group representatives attended the annual assemblies. Throughout the period from the early 1980's to today, the Northern California Conferences and now the area conventions include full participation of the Alateen members. The teens plan their own convention agenda, often include Al-Anon members in open Alateen meetings and contribute speakers to the Al-Anon program.

In 1996, the World Service Conference approved an experiment that would change the structure of the World Service Office and the delegate committees. As part of this experiment, they established an Alateen Advisory Committee responsible to the Group Services Director. This committee includes participation of teens from everywhere in the US. Two teens, sisters from Castro Valley, were selected to be part of that committee for a one-year term in 1998.

Notes

[1] Bob S. Jr. and his sister Sue W. are the children of Bob S., co-founder of AA and Annie Smith. He shared at an event in San Jose in August, 2000.

[2] *Children of the Healer*, p 101. Reprinted with permission of the Hazelden Foundation.

[3] While this is not technically correct, (because an Alateen is a child younger than 21 who attends Alateen meetings), it reflects his wish today that he had listened to his parents.

[4] The letter isn't written on AFG Headquarters stationery, but we can presume that this letter came from their office.

[5] The Alcoholic Foundation eventually became known as AA World Services, Inc.

[6] The National Committee on Alcoholism, founded by Marty M., one of the first women in AA, eventually became known as the National Council on Alcoholism and Drug Dependence (NCADD).

[7] Letter to Mrs. Doyle R. of New Castle Indiana was printed in *First Steps*, p 71. Reprinted with permission of AFG Headquarters, Inc.

[8] *First Steps*, p 100. Reprinted with permission of AFG Headquarters, Inc.

[9] *It's a Teenaged Affair*, P-10 by AFG Headquarters, Inc. The pamphlet was discontinued in 1999.

[10] The AA Grapevine, Inc. publishes the *Grapevine* magazine.

[11] *First Steps*, p 103. Reprinted with permission of Al-Anon Family Group Headquarters, Inc.

[12] Al-Anon Clearing House and AFG Headquarters seem to have been used interchangeably during this period.

[13] Randy T. was then a UC Berkeley student from Southern California.

[14] Themes and a description of the logo for each year of NoCAC are listed earlier in this chapter.

[15] Friends Outside is an organization devoted to serving prisoners and families of inmates.

[16] These youngsters were convicted and sentenced to the facility. As many as 250 residents at a time, they ranged in age from 9 to 18. About 7,000 youngsters pass through the facility yearly. "Many come from families where one or both parents are chemically dependent."

[17] The Bill Wilson Center is a county operated juvenile home for teens.

[18] This is the Board of Trustees for Al-Anon Family Group Headquarters, Inc.

[19] The Al-Anon Alateen Information (AA/I) committee was formed from this sponsors workshop and continues to be active through the year 2000.

[20] This coordinator attended her first Preteen Alateen meeting in 1980 in San Jose at the age of 6 1/2.

[21] *Guide for Sponsors of Alateen Groups*, P-29, is available from Al-Anon Family Group Headquarters, Inc.

[22] *Alateen, Hope for Children of Alcoholics*, B-3, was first published by Al-Anon Family Group Headquarters, Inc. in 1973.

[23] These guidelines formed the basis of some of the topics found in A *Guide to Alateen Sponsorship—an Unforgettable Adventure*, P-86, published by Al-Anon Family Group Headquarters, Inc.

7

Other Communities and Cultures

Diversity has different meanings depending on who is discussing the topic. One might think that the First Tradition's statement, "personal progress for the greatest number depends upon unity," could mean that the program and its occupants are the same. It, however, is more complex. Unity depends upon our adherence to our primary purpose, which is defined as, "to help families of alcoholics."[1] While we believe that most early Al-Anon meetings were "wives' groups," it wasn't long before others affected by someone else's drinking showed up at the doors of Al-Anon. Men have been involved from the beginning. George S. of Loomis was not only involved in his own personal recovery. He also chaired the first organizing committee that became known as the Northern California Al-Anon Council in 1952. The Spanish speaking communities followed in their husband's AA footsteps and formed Al-Anon meetings as early as 1968. This chapter devotes itself primarily to the advent of men in the program, the Gay and Lesbian community, the Adult Child movement and how our area reached out to immigrants from other countries, primarily the Russian and Indian communities. Other chapters discuss involvement with the Hispanic community and with Alateen.

Early Alcoholics Anonymous experiences

All of the very early members of the fledgling program of Alcoholics Anonymous were men. Smitty[2] is quoted as describing his father's thoughts about women. "He didn't know how to handle them."[3] In AA's second year, a man came to an AA group and said he was the "victim of another addiction even worse stigmatized than alcoholism." The group's "oldest member"[4] spoke in confidence with two others. They discussed "the trouble this strange alcoholic might bring" and the notion that it might be better to "sacrifice this one for the sake of many." Finally, one of the three said, "What we are really afraid of is our reputation." And he asked a question that had been haunting him: "What would the Master do?" No answer was necessary."[5] A gay man was allowed to find sobriety in AA. This was the way the early recovering alcoholics began to accept that other problems would not interfere with their primary purpose. "The only requirement for AA member-ship is an honest desire to stop drinking."[6]

Women also joined AA to find sobriety. At first the wives of AA members were furious that their husbands would continue to be around the same women they had seen and flirted with at the bars. "Bill recalled 'explosions' that took place around the 'out-of-bounds romance' and the arrival of alcoholic women at meetings. Women alcoholics had to overcome a double standard that was even more rigid in the 1930's— the notion that nice women didn't drink to excess."[7] In Cleveland, "Warren C. re-membered that the first woman was thrown out of AA by the wives."[8]

"The idea that men should help men and women should help women evolved as a means of AA self-preservation, before experience proved it wise for the new-comers' sake. The only trouble was that there were so few women AA's to help the women. So the wives continued to do the job."[9] And so it appears that the wives of alcoholics were still working with their husbands and now with the alcoholic wives to help them obtain sobriety.

Early Al-Anon Experiences

Lois W. shared about how the early wives were part of the Oxford Group meetings and that they eventually became aware that the principles laid out by AA might be applicable to themselves. She describes her own experience in New York where the AA group didn't allow the wives to attend. "Therefore, while they met in the as-sembly room below, a handful of us wives got to know each other in the skylighted studio above. It was great to find that because others had gone through similar experiences, each of us no longer had to be alone with our troubles. Our family gatherings were composed mostly of AA wives, with a sprinkling of mothers and daughters. There was one man, Wally S., a father who was trying to get his son into AA."[10] "It was Bill who suggested to Wally that he should encourage his son, then a young adult to become independent. After many near disasters, the son joined AA. Many parents of young alcoholics who are members of Al-Anon will relate to Wally's dilemma as a parent."[11]

Al-Anon Men in Northern California

George S. of Loomis shares how he went to his first AA meeting with his wife before 1949. He began attending non-alcoholic meetings in Sacramento as soon as one was available. In December 1952, he attended the Northern California AA Council Conference in San Rafael, where the spouses met briefly to begin organizing. He was elected chairman. Andy from Oakland was elected vice-chairman. In 1951, Ray C. of San Jose went to one meeting with three or four wives in Salinas, CA. He came back to Al-Anon in 1956. In 1971, he shared, "I was alone in a world of despair. At first I went to AA meetings with my wife for moral support and then my sponsor suggested I go to Al-Anon. I met other men whose wives had a drinking problem, but I was very uncomfortable with all those women. One woman had caused a lot of trouble, so why should a man feel that more women could help him? Little did I know how good these meetings were for me! Resentment was replaced with acceptance and forgiveness, fear was replaced by faith in a Higher Power and faith in myself, bitterness was replaced by gratitude and loneliness by the friendship of the many wonderful members of Al-Anon."[12] Ray, along with two other men, started a men's group in San Jose around 1964. It went on for about ten years, and then it faded. Al M., a long time member from San Jose, shared that he attended this meeting, which met at the welfare building on Younger Avenue. By 1975, there were two Stag meetings listed in the area group summary, one in District VI, (now 13) and one in District VII, (now 14).

In the fall of 1964, the Northern California Conference had an interesting schedule, with mostly men as chairs of the individual sessions. This is a copy of that agenda:

9:30 AM Sat	Workshop	John C. San Jose
11:00 AM	World Services	John F. San Jose
1:00 PM	Meeting	Chair: Ray C. San Jose
	Speaker	Bob I. Fresno
2:30	Business Meeting	Election of Officers
3:30 PM	Alateen Meeting	Host: San Jose Alateen Group
11:00 AM Sun	Meeting	Chair: Del M. Sacramento
		Speaker: Ray C. San Jose

John F. of San Jose was the district committeeman from San Jose in 1963. At this assembly the decision was implemented to divide California into two areas. At the election of officers, he became the first assembly chairman.

Bob J. of Sacramento believes that the Sacramento Men's Group is the oldest continuous men's meeting in Al-Anon. He shared, "Our first meeting was on July 17, 1977, and for the first 12 years our meeting was 'open ended,' with many of them lasting until almost midnight."

Today 17 Men's groups are registered with the area. Interestingly, there are only 13 registered women's groups.

Gay and Lesbian Groups

The Whitman-Radclyffe Foundation asked in a questionnaire, "Do you believe homosexuality is an illness?" The San Francisco district replied, "Dear Mr. S_, We are returning your questionnaire unanswered. While we are gratified to learn of your concern & work for Alcoholics of the Homosexual Community, it would be a violation of our 10th Tradition to express a group opinion on an outside issue such as homosexuality. We can, however, wish you much success."

Bud B. was one of the original members of the earliest known gay-identified Al-Anon group in San Francisco. Bud and some friends started the Tuesday Night Gay Men's and Women's AFG in 1975 at the Acceptance House on the north side of Golden Gate Avenue near Divisadero. Today it is named the Tuesday Night Gay Lesbian Bisexual AFG. This location was the first gay halfway house.

A long-time member, Glynn D., shares, "For the first two years of my recovery, my home group was identified as a gay and lesbian AFG. It was important for me to know that when members shared about personal relationships and family problems involving sexuality, these topics were not off-limits in meetings. It's frightening to think where I would be now if I had not thought I was welcome to the fellowship completely, as I was. Today I share my program with all sorts of people, people honestly seeking to address their problems in a life of ongoing spiritual discovery. My present home group focuses on the 11th Step, but I'm glad that meetings identified as gay or lesbian exist. I continue to meet gay and lesbian newcomers whose fear of judgment can be a barrier to their getting to know our fellowship. The particular welcome to gays and lesbians in our literature is especially reassuring to many of us. A natural branching out from gay or lesbian identified groups to other groups is common among the members I know. Each of the four gay and lesbian identified groups of which I have been a member has asserted that the meetings are open to all. We want to apply the 3rd Tradition in the case of folks with any declared sexual preference or none, as with all other things."

The Living Sober Recovery Conference is an annual event held in San Francisco, hosted by gay, lesbian, bisexual and transgender members of Alcoholics Anonymous, with Al-Anon participation. The first annual conference was held in the summer of 1976, and its 25th conference in the summer of 2000. Living Sober has gone from participation of a few hundred to more than 5,500. More recently, it has settled to about 2,000 people. Al-Anon has participated since 1988. Conferences are usually held on the weekend nearest July 4, and the ongoing conference committee can be contacted at the web site *www.livingsober.org.*

Adult Children

An early member from Santa Clara shares his experience when he came to his first Al-Anon meeting in 1983. "My very first Al-Anon meeting was in a classroom at a parochial school. It was, as I later came to find out, a normal meeting. There were fewer than a dozen people there, all middle-aged women, with the feel of weariness and martyrdom in their married life. I remember their broad backsides wedged into the student desks, and thinking this was not for me. A month or two later, however, I came back to Al-Anon, but this time it was to a meeting with a focus on those raised in an alcoholic home, an ACA[13] meeting. It was a packed room, jumping with energy, mostly younger professionals, and a mixture of men and women, many if not most, were single. I was utterly alienated. I had not had a friend in years. Although I was married, I was estranged and distant from my wife and very alone and isolated within the world. My life seemed purposeless, meaningless. I came back to the meeting the next week. A woman came right up to me and welcomed me back by name. I had not been invited anywhere in many years, and it was so touching to have someone glad to see me."

In March 1977, the WSO noted, "Children who are exposed to alcoholic parents are severely handicapped emotionally, spiritually and often physically. The children suffer from the erratic behavior of the non-alcoholic often as much, if not more, than that of the alcoholic. The stigma of alcoholism often prevents the spouse of the alcoholic from seeking help. As a result, the children may be severely damaged... Al-Anon offers a constructive, spiritually based program by which its members learn to achieve peace of mind and a more rational approach to life and its problems."[14]

The WSO recognized that children were affected by both parents' behaviors, and in this Public Information bulletin, continued to focus on helping parents by helping them understand the damage caused to their children by this disease.

In 1982, Claudia Black and other therapists formed an organization called the National Association for Children of Alcoholics (NACOA) in Southern California. There was a national conference for counselors, therapists and other professionals held in Florida the following year. Bob S. Jr.[15] recalls the confusion in the minds of the Al-Anon staff as they tried to understand this new primarily professional movement. The conference was loaded with professionals who were eager to learn how they could help those whose parents had too much to drink. The WSO reported in 1982, "Somehow we have to get across the ideas that all types of members are included in the literature."[16]

Dr. Claudia Black shared her professional story in *Al-Anon Faces Alcoholism*. Her article encourages adults who have alcoholic parents to attend Al-Anon meetings. "These are adults who characteristically experience greater difficulty in their ability to trust, to identify and express feelings and ask for what they need."[17] Many of these adults were not happy to sit in meetings where they were reminded of their parent's behavior, nor were the parents willing to listen to others who reminded them that they didn't treat their own children properly. She urged Al-Anon to focus on the child's story rather than the parents' behavior.

The early member continues, "In Santa Clara County, Al-Anon meetings with an ACA focus were very new and very large. Some meetings exceeded 100 people a week. There was no conference approved literature supportive of ACA issues, so many meetings took a group conscience and brought in outside literature dealing with co-dependence, ACA, and other related topics. Much of the growth in new members came from therapists who had clinically identified various patterns of dysfunction in those raised within an alcoholic environment. They consistently recommended Al-Anon and ACA to their patients. Moreover, several authors of ACA books and leading therapists began holding profitable conventions and conferences for ACA's. Attendance at these events would often exceed a thousand people. There was a huge explosion of interest in ACA meetings, especially after these conventions.

"Given the size of the meetings and the rapid growth, there were not enough sponsors, and very little talk of real solutions. ACA meetings were often emotional, and often profound, much more intense than the typical Al-Anon meeting."

A member of the Joy of Living Al-Anon Group in San Jose, meeting at a recovery facility, reports that in the mid 1980's there were four types of meeting on the facility's bulletin board, Al-Anon, ACOA (12 weeks of classes) ACOA (with long term therapy) and an Al-Anon meeting with Adult Child focus that called itself an ACA meeting. Eventually, the World Service Office asked adult child focused groups to refer to themselves as Al-Anon Adult Children Groups (AAC) so as to reduce the confusion that occurred as a result of all the initials used in this movement.

Some ACA groups joined the ACA organization. In Stockton and Sacramento, the ACA groups banded together and voted to be separate from Al-Anon. In the Bay Area, most of the groups voted to become part of the Al-Anon structure. Kathleen D. reported, "District 14[18] had only one Al-Anon 'ACA' meeting that left Al-Anon and really affiliated with ACA. They wanted to use all sorts of literature, and didn't want to limit themselves to Al-Anon Conference Approved Literature."

The early member continues, "ACA meetings often had sharing about sexual or physical abuse of members when they were children, I never heard these topics broached at mainstream meetings. Sexuality, in all its varieties, and the progress in one's significant relationship was often spoken of at length in ACA meetings, and almost never at meeting level in mainstream Al-Anon meetings. Issues around food, money, shopping, debiting, etc. were frequently explored in ACA meetings.

"When we tried to share these topics in mainstream meetings, we were often met with the reply that these should be talked about in private, not at meeting level. However, the core affliction of an ACA is denial, and keeping family secrets is a part of that denial process. (This may be why mainstream Al-Anon members did not want us to speak up). Most ACA's believed that, for healing to occur, required the identification of the personal consequences of alcoholism, and that common understanding would lead to healing."

Al-Anon Family Group Headquarters, Inc. and the World Service Conference faced a giant spiritual challenge to accommodate people who were reaching out for recovery from growing up with the affects of someone else's alcoholism in the home. There was never a question of whether members from these new type meetings qualified for Al-Anon. They did qualify. Components of the challenge were: 1) How to keep the Al-Anon program free from professionalism; 2) keep and hold on to the long standing agreement initiated by Lois W. and Anne B. never to discuss any kind of sexual abuse, a completely private matter, during meetings; and 3) to produce high quality pieces of Al-Anon literature coming from the shared experience of members through the Conference Approved Literature process.

By 1986, the World Service Conference approved a motion welcoming adult children into Al-Anon. It reads, "In the spirit of unity, the 1986 World Service Conference affirms its long standing welcome to adult children of alcoholics. We acknowledge the need they have expressed for the Al-Anon program of recovery."[19] Some years later, the WSO began publishing literature with more of an ACA focus, such as *In All Our Affairs*[20] and *From Survival to Recovery*.[21] In the works is a daily reader[22] with the focus on childhood issues.

In 1988, a cover story about *Alcohol and the Family* in the weekly news magazine, *Newsweek*,[23] mentions the efforts of several professionals (and their books) and how many of these professionals urged their patients to attend Al-Anon ACA meetings. "The 14 Al-Anon affiliated groups in the early '80s have increased to 1,100." It continues, "The 7 million children of alcoholics who are under the age of 18 are harder to help, if only because their parents' denial tends to keep them out of treatment."

The early member continued, "In those early days, one or two of the vanguard ACA members sponsored a half dozen "babies" as they were called. However, very few of the babies sponsored a third generation, and thus the recovery in ACA did not sustain itself or grow. My first two or three sponsors were ACA men with very little recovery themselves, and it did not work out. Then I chose a sponsor with lots of recovery from mainstream Al-Anon. He never dwelled on the differences in our paths, and accepted me, even as estranged from mainstream Al-Anon as I was. His love and acceptance helped me heal my own rift with Al-Anon, and with my alcoholic father.

"Gradually, attendance at ACA meetings dwindled. Some meetings folded and some shifted to a more traditional format with a little ACA focus. As the ACA members aged and matured in the program, more and more took on service positions, and began to be assimilated into the mainstream of Al-Anon. We began to see more of the similarity between the typical Al-Anon members and ourselves.

"I began to have more compassion for my parents, both the active drinker and the spouse. Forgiveness became more important to me than identifying the issues. I passed through the healing steps, and as I did so, the fire inside softened. I reached the amends steps, and came at the whole endeavor with more love and acceptance. I began to be grateful in a general way for Al-Anon, and left behind the clamor of the ACA meetings/program."

At the area level today, there are 29 Al-Anon groups with Adult Child focus registered in thirteen districts.

Diversity Days

Diversity Day began because some Northern California members believed that more outreach needed to be done for and with other cultures and communities. One member repeatedly insisted that Al-Anon outreach be broadened. Then another member picked up the cry, and another and another. We were reminded that almost 50% of the population in California is not Caucasian and were from a variety of religious backgrounds.

At the Redding Assembly in 1997, the idea for a diversity day was first mentioned. At the October 1997 Northern California World Service Committee meeting in San Mateo, the preparations were made to host a day of workshops to discuss diversity. During the planning meetings, the workshop became known as Diversity Day. The first Diversity Day was held on April 25, 1998 in Berkeley. Two thirds of the attendees were from the Spanish Al-Anon meetings. The delegate, Cathy C., placed a world map in the lobby and asked each person who attended to identify their country of origin. What a surprise to see all six continents represented and almost 30 countries!

Since the Spanish members had already overcome so many barriers, they shared their experience, strength and hope with the rest of us. The leaders asked, "How do we reach other cultures and communities?" The underlying question asked was, "Can I step out of my comfort zone, overcome my fears and anxieties and extend my hand to help those from other cultures and communities?"

Newcomers, especially from a foreign land, get frightened when they go to an Al-Anon meeting in a church, listen to the Al-Anon steps, many of which have the word "God" in them, and watch the members close the meetings with the Lord's Prayer. Religious people are fearful that they may have to face their religion or leave their own. A non-Christian might think Al-Anon is a way to convert them to Christianity. We Al-Anon members know this is not the case. But the newcomers don't. At the Diversity Day, we asked ourselves: "Whom are we trying to help?" The answer was "the newcomer who is afraid." We asked, "What can we change?"

Diversity Day taught us to consider the following: 1) meetings in one's native tongue are vital, as it is the language of the heart, 2) to welcome these new members personally, honor their differences and accept them and 3) be patient, love them unconditionally and 4) consider not using the Lord's Prayer to close the meeting.

We discovered there are several keys to success. The most important is learning that when someone feels different, they reach out to their own communities' traditional support, whether it is the Al-Anon member from another country, with a different sexual preference, a physical disability or anything that they believe makes them different. Al-Anon can support those communities as newcomers begin their alcoholism recovery process. Al-Anon members can support that newcomer in an infinite number of ways, such as sponsoring an Al-Anon group with that focus, distributing posters about the Al-Anon meeting to their crisis centers, contributing literature to their clubs and other places where they congregate and sharing at their Al-Anon meetings, since many do understand some English.

Other members shared that since the beginning of the Al-Anon program, Al-Anon groups have sponsored other types of meeting like Alateen, Institutions and another meeting at a different time. Al-Anon members can consider supporting another type of meeting, such as a meeting for another culture. District and Al-

Anon Information Services added "Cultural Outreach" to their district agenda to talk about how to reach other cultures and communities on a regular basis.

As our insight expanded, the name of the area coordinator has changed. In 1988 the area approved a new coordinator position called Spanish-Speaking Co-ordinator because the number of Spanish meetings were just beginning to grow. In the next three years 30 new Spanish meetings were formed. In 1991, the name of the coordinator was changed to Non-English Speaking so that outreach could be extended to newcomers who spoke other languages. The coordinators kept a list-ing of bilingual members willing to be speakers in other languages and made the list available throughout the area. In 2000, the name changed again to become the Diversity Coordinator in order to support not only newcomers and groups in other languages, but those whose culture are different from the typical Al-Anon meeting participants.

The Russian Community

In 1991, the Iron Curtain fell. The Soviet Union collapsed and freedom was intro-duced into the various provinces. Many of these provinces became separate and new countries. It was an exciting time for Alcoholics Anonymous and Al-Anon. During the Soviet regime, alcoholism was officially a crime. Now there was a chance that new ideas could take hold. AA was in the forefront and Al-Anon was working beside them, visiting the universities and the government institutions to help in establishing local meetings, translating the AA Big Book and Al-Anon literature such as the *One Day at a Time in Al-Anon*. Because there was no Al-Anon structure in Russia, there was no organization to receive translation rights. Because there was no currency exchange, it was not possible to sell literature to local groups and individuals. The World Service Office proposed that areas "adopt a group" and be responsible for purchasing and mailing literature to the groups in the former So-viet Union. Individual Al-Anon groups, districts and AIS's adopted Russian groups. Some groups mailed their literature directly to the group, including sharings, jour-nals, bookmarks, postcards, and even stamps. Some Russian groups responded and expressed their heartfelt gratitude.

Don R. shares how he helped two Al-Anon meetings in Magadan, which is on the coast of the Sea of Okhotsk, in Russia directly north of Japan. "On July 4, 1992, I met a group of actors and singers at my church that were on a reciprocal visit from Magadan. I had an interest in carrying the message to Russia due to the extreme need there. So I tried to make some contact with the Russians. They didn't speak English, and I didn't speak Russian. They had one translator for about 24 people. I was finally able to capture the translator for a while. A woman indi-cated a desire to assist families of alcoholics in Magadan. Peggy C., our Al-Anon delegate, offered me the only copy in Northern California of the newly released Russian ODAT. I gave it to this woman. She gave me her business card but I never heard from her. I was finally able to contact an American Catholic priest via e-mail as a result of a message from a member in Alaska. The priest had about three AA meetings in his church. Due to mistrust the people in Magadan had for each other, AA meetings consisted only of two to three members who knew each other. He eventually sent me a message telling me there were three women looking over his shoulder as he was typing a message to me. They wanted to start an Al-Anon meeting. Coincidentally, about three weeks previously, I had sent a fairly good-sized quantity of various Al-Anon pamphlets and books to the parents of a young Russian woman who was then a member of my church. She and her husband carried the literature to Magadan in their luggage and arrived a few days before that e-mail message from the priest. After they brought the literature to the church, it didn't take long for two groups in Magadan to register."

The area committee appointed Don R. as the "Adopt-A-Group Contact" in 1996. The group assigned to our area was the Near Fireside Group in Salavat, a city of over 2 million about 800 miles southeast of Moscow. In 2000, this responsibility was included at part of the Diversity Coordinator's position. There are many Russian immigrants in Eureka, part of District 1. These individuals offered to and helped the World Service Office in assuring that the translations accurately described the Al-Anon approach to healing into Russian.

Immigrants from India and Afghanistan

At the April 10, 1999 Diversity Day, one of the members shared her experience in starting a new meeting. She was born in India, speaks Hindi and Punjabi, and was willing to start a meeting. In the East Bay, there is a huge community of people from India. Her meeting's group conscience was to make a one-year minimum commitment to support the Indian group. Both meet at the same time and share the facility, literature and refreshments. In order to attract new members, posters were distributed to the public libraries, the Indian grocery stores and temples. An Indian TV station based in New York City aired the "Tornado" Public Service Announcement in California and our three neighboring states. Members provided posters, district meeting lists and Al-Anon literature to the Southeast Asian battered women's shelter, as their clients were eligible to attend the new meeting. Members from her meeting volunteered to drive women to and from the shelter. Some women from the shelter were from other countries, for instance, Afghanistan, so a member from Iran who spoke Farsi helped them. The two keys mentioned previously, the bilingual member and her home group, made this outreach possible. Outreach to other cultures and communities is not difficult; it just takes a little longer and, now the area has a working outreach model!

Notes

[1] Al-Anon's fifth Tradition. Reprinted with permission of AA World Services, Inc. and AFG Headquarters, Inc.

[2] Smitty was the common nickname for Bob S., the son of the co-founder of AA, Dr. Bob S.

[3] *Dr. Bob and the Good Oldtimers*, p 241. Reprinted with permission of AA World Services, Inc.

[4] Bill W. identified the "oldest member" in the 1960's as Dr. Bob, his co-founder.

[5] *Dr Bob and the Good Oldtimers*, p 240-241. Reprinted with permission of AA World Services, Inc.

[6] The third Tradition of AA. Reprinted with permission of AA World Services, Inc.

[7] *Dr. Bob and the Good Oldtimers*, p 241. Reprinted with permission of AA World Services, Inc.

[8] *Dr. Bob and the Good Oldtimers*, p 241. Reprinted with permission of AA World Services, Inc.

[9] *Dr. Bob and the Good Oldtimers*, p 243. Reprinted with permission of Alcoholics Anonymous World Services, Inc.

[10] *Lois Remembers*, p 172. Reprinted with permission of AFG Headquarters, Inc.

[11] *First Steps, Al-Anon 35 Years of Beginnings*, p 114. Reprinted with permission of AFG Headquarters, Inc.

[12] *Al-Anon Twelve Stepper*, March 1971. Reprinted with permission of NCWSA.

[13] ACA is one acronym for an Al-Anon meeting with an Adult Child of an Alcoholic focus.

[14] *The Influence of Al-Anon on Children of Alcoholics*, PI-29; 3/77. Reprinted with permission of AFG Headquarters, Inc.

[15] Bob S. Jr., son of AA co-founder Bob S., was a featured speaker at this conference.

[16] *1982 World Service Conference Summary*, p 31. Reprinted with permission of AFG Headquarters, Inc.

[17] *Al-Anon Faces Alcoholism*, Second Edition 1984, p 63. Reprinted with permission of Al-Anon Family Group Headquarters, Inc.

[18] For District 14 boundaries, see the district maps.

[19] *1986 World Service Conference Summary*, p 46. Published with permission of AFG Headquarters, Inc.

[20] *In All Our Affairs*, B-15, published in 1989 by AFG Headquarters, Inc.

[21] *From Survival to Recovery*, B-21, published in 1994 by AFG Headquarters, Inc.

[22] Publication of a daily reader was approved in 1997.

[23] *Newsweek*, January 18, 1988, p 62 etc.

8

Area Controversies

Controversy is part of life. Al-Anon members are no exception; they too enter into controversial issues. In fact our committee had spirited discussions as to which controversies to address. Finally, we focused on four enduring controversies: professional terms, the use of prayer, crosstalk, and the rights and responsibilities of dual members. Other hot topics, such as changes in the literature and personalities in Al-Anon were considered, but are addressed in other chapters.

Professional Terms

Professional terms have been used in our program since the Al-Anon program was founded in 1951. It took a while to digest the true meaning of Tradition Six, "lend our name to any outside enterprise" and Eight, "Twelfth Step work should remain forever nonprofessional". It seems inevitable that professional terms continue to find their way into Al-Anon. One difficulty is in recognizing that a term is a professional term. Using professional terms confuse newcomers. An Al-Anon member using a professional term may not know what it means, adding to the confusion. It seems more prudent to share what our behavior is rather than use a professional term we might not understand ourselves. Today, the service manual is positive about this topic. It says, "Focus on the Al-Anon interpretation of our program is strengthened when we avoid using professional terms and labels."[1] Some terms that have been used over the years are described below, but certainly this is not a complete list.

"Terms such as para-alcoholic, near-alcoholic, co-alcoholic or other professional jargon can confuse and sometimes conflict with the Al-Anon message of recovery."[2] These terms listed in that early service manual are not often heard at meetings today, but new ones have been found to take their place.

One of those is "codependent". Codependent became common when a book with the word in its title became a best seller. The use of this word was a mixed blessing. The author of the book dedicated a chapter discussing the importance of Al-Anon and Alateen in recovery and recommended that readers attend meetings. The author was successful. Many "codependent" members came and stayed. On one hand, Al-Anon members spent much effort in describing their own recovery in non-technical language and trying to avoid using the word "codependent." On the other hand, the term became part of the common every day language. It is included in some of Al-Anon's latest literature and is no longer difficult to understand.

ACA, the acronym for "Adult Children of Alcoholics", was an even more difficult term for Al-Anon. One member shares about his confusion: "I attended an Al-Anon meeting in a treatment center where the various meetings were listed on the bulletin board. The meetings at this location were: Al-Anon, ACOA (a 12 week therapy session) ACOA (a long-term therapy session), and an Adult Child Al-Anon Group. In addition, there were ACA and ACOA 12 step groups forming throughout the county. There were at least four different forms of ACA. Which one was the right one?" He learned that all were correct, but only one was part of Al-Anon. It became obvious that the suggestions of long time members became very important, that we use the words, adult child of an alcoholic or adult with alcoholic parents, not the various acronyms and describe our difficulty in growing up with the disease of alcoholism. There is a complete discussion of the role of the adult child of an alcoholic in Al-Anon in chapter 7 about other cultures and communities.

The term, "dysfunctional family", began circulating within Al-Anon in the 1990's. This seems to refer to the actions a family takes in reaction to the active drinker, including the drinker's actions, and also to the actions of the family that occur even when alcohol is no longer present in the home. The problem with this term is that it is difficult to find someone who knows what a "functional family" is. Since there is no easy definition of either type of family, the use of the term doesn't impart any knowledge of the family situation. One member of Al-Anon shares, "I heard an AA convention speaker (who claimed to be a professional in the alcohol field and a preacher) suggest that "dysfunctional family" was badly used in the alcoholism recovery communities. As he shared, he told of his reading the Bible for guidance. He found several instances where families were described. He settled on the first family who had two children, one of whom killed the other. He concluded that with family examples like this, there is little hope of finding an example of a "functional family." The term is not commonly used in the Al-Anon literature and is still considered a professional term.

The term, "intervention" is used as part of the medical solutions to alcoholism. Many times an Al-Anon member who is frustrated with their loved one's continued drinking asks if an "intervention" should be done. This is a method used in an attempt to "hurry the alcoholic's bottom" and force sobriety on an alcoholic. Al-Anon does not profess to be a clearinghouse for various methods of alcoholism treatment. While individual members might be professionals in the field, Al-Anon itself is careful to preserve its traditions by not trying to describe or recommend any particular form of treatment. When the Al-Anon fellowship takes sides as to which type of treatment is good or bad, this action leads to controversy among the professionals, and when it becomes public, can only hinder referrals that help families of alcoholics. Al-Anon members eventually learn to take care of themselves and to leave medical advice between the alcoholic and his or her doctor or counselor.

Crosstalk

In recent years, probably since the late 1980's, there has been increasing discussions among members about individuals "cross talking" during meetings. While the complaints have continued, there hasn't been any agreement as to what the term itself means. An Al-Anon member from Eureka writes, "In our area, there is much concern over crosstalk and it is my opinion there is a great misunderstanding what crosstalk is." [3] Another member, from San Francisco, said, "When I speak at a meeting, I'm serving as an open channel for my Higher Power to speak through me… If you feel moved by what you hear, that's a function of your openness to the message your Higher Power has for you… Keep it principle-centered, leaving me out of it." [4]

An *Inside Al-Anon* article itself asks "Is It Loving Interchange or Crosstalk?" Loving interchange is defined as helping someone who states a problem when others share how they handle a similar situation. A sharing in the *Dilemma of the Alcoholic Marriage* gives an example of loving interchange. In this book, the meeting chairperson describes a situation at their home and asks, "What should I do?" The members go around the room and share ideas they've tried in similar situations. On the opposite side are those who believe referring to someone else's share during the time they share themselves is objectionable, just the opposite of the sharing in the *Dilemma*. A member from Chico is concerned about this latter view. "If no one responds, including the chair/leader, after the sharing of an emotionally upset member or newcomer, the meeting turns icy cold right then. It used to be that after anyone talked, another member could be helpful by sharing a similar experience with a member/newcomer."

Others have defined crosstalk as two members holding an open conversation with each other to the exclusion of the rest of the group, or two members having a side whispering conversation while another person speaks. Crosstalk is one of those issues in Al-Anon where there appears to be no common definition or resolution. Some groups try to define it and describe their opinion as part of their opening statements.

Prayers in Al-Anon and Alateen Groups

Most Al-Anon and Alateen groups in Northern California followed the original pattern established by Alcoholics Anonymous by opening with the Serenity Prayer[5] and closing with the Lord's Prayer.

The 1974 World Service Conference approved the use of "Let It Begin With Me" declaration. The WSO Policy[6] Committee proposed this declaration as a revision of the AA's "I Am Responsible"[7] statement. There are many other prayers listed in Conference Approved Literature, the most familiar ones being the Serenity Prayer and the prayer on the "Just For Today"[8] bookmark attributed to St. Francis of Assisi.

In the late 1980's and early 1990's there was an upwelling of objections to the use of the Lord's Prayer at Northern California Assemblies. At the 1989 assembly, a motion to change the closing prayer from the Lord's Prayer to the Serenity Prayer failed. But at the 1990 assembly[9] the members voted to close with the Serenity Prayer.

At the 1991 assembly, a controversy erupted around the prayer issue. The printed agenda showed that the discussion of the prayer issue would take place on Saturday afternoon. It was actually discussed early in the morning. Some group representatives who were interested in this issue were not present when the first discussion was conducted. The morning motion[10] was passed as follows: "That we close the meeting with the Lord's Prayer as usual." In the afternoon, after an appeal by those group representatives who were not present in the morning, there was more discussion, (sometimes heated). A new motion was made to close with both the Lord's Prayer and the Serenity Prayer. There was no vote on this motion. A consensus was taken to close the meeting with the Lord's Prayer. In spite of the chair's declaration of a consensus, a second circle of attendees formed outside the room and recited the Serenity Prayer while the remainder closed as the chairperson requested. On Sunday, a third motion to close with the Serenity Prayer failed.

A participant shared her feelings about the experience, "I remember a long discussion about the Lord's Prayer. Many were for saying it and some were offended and angry that they were forced to say it. One of the meetings of the assembly closed with many angry members storming out of the room and shouting their closing prayer as the rest closed with the Lord's Prayer inside. Another meeting closed with 10 to 20 members going to the front of the room by the dais. Some left the dais to join the circle in the front of the room. I was so confused. The disunity was so upsetting. My heart ached with sadness and fear for our program. I didn't join the other circle but I also didn't say the Lord's Prayer."

A "brainstorming session" was conducted at the next area committee (NCWSC) meeting in an attempt to find an answer to this emotionally charged and divisive controversy. The committee members were asked to submit every prayer that any member of the committee thought might be appropriate. After receiving over ten suggestions, the committee voted on the ones they preferred. After the first ballot, those prayers that didn't receive a vote were eliminated. In successive votes, the prayer with the lowest vote count was also eliminated. When the list was reduced to four choices, one committee member suggested the idea of using all four choices. The committee agreed and voted to place the Serenity Prayer, the Lord's Prayer, the Al-Anon Declaration and the Moment of Silence on cards and to choose one prayer from a hat each time a prayer was appropriate. They also agreed to continue this practice for the next few meetings and see if these choices might be healing. This practice has been used since 1991 at area committee (NCWSC) meetings and assemblies. The 1997 assembly formally approved this practice.[11]

Rights and Responsibilities of Dual Members

At almost every assembly, the issue of who is qualified to serve beyond the group level is discussed with varying concerns for individuals and sometimes with heated outbursts. A dual member is defined as a person who states that he or she is a member both of Alcoholics Anonymous and Al-Anon. The policy does not refer to other twelve step programs because Al-Anon has no special ties to them. The policy also does not refer to someone who may need to stop drinking but isn't a member of AA. The current policy of the World Service Conference is quite clear as stated in the Service Manual. It says in part, "Because of the unique nature of both programs, Al-Anon/Alateen members who are also AA members do not hold office beyond the group level, as these positions could lead to membership in the World Service Conference."[12] The 1987 NCWSA Assembly Dual Member Policy is more specific for area positions. It says in part, "...a dual member cannot hold any position which would affect more than one group since this would indeed place that person 'above the group level'"[13].

This was not an issue before Al-Anon was formed. Prior to 1951, spouses of AA members often assisted the AA groups by supplying coffee and refreshments, sometimes even serving as officers in the AA group.[14] These same persons were those who began to see the wisdom in applying the AA principles to their own lives. Alcoholics Anonymous was already denying entrance to "non-alcoholics" during the 1940's. While they collected information about non-alcoholic groups, the AA Clearing House didn't register any groups that were for non-alcoholics.

After 1951, it was understood that AA members went to AA and Al-Anon members went to Al-Anon Family Groups. An early question[15] was, "Could the alcoholic wife of an AA member attend Al-Anon meetings?" The answer said she was eligible to attend an Al-Anon meeting, but the group might not be willing to invite her to stay because her "presence inhibits the group and prevents free discussion."

In 1969 the World Service Conference acknowledged that members of Alcoholics Anonymous could be members of Al-Anon because their own lives have or had been affected by someone else's alcoholism, even though their own lives were directly affected by their own alcoholism. In 1976, the World Service Conference established the current policy listed above. Various motions to the floor have been presented at several World Service Conferences since then. Each time the WSC has reaffirmed this policy.[16]

Statements of those opposed to the current policy center around the need for service workers and the ability of dual members to understand how to differentiate between their AA and Al-Anon programs. Those in favor of the current policy believe that there is an inherent conflict of interest when a member of AA becomes involved in Al-Anon service and in establishing Al-Anon policy. Many also believe that the current policy should remain intact to maintain and respect the part of Tradition Six that identifies that Al-Anon is a separate entity from Alcoholics Anonymous. This is because the Alcoholics Anonymous fellowship itself insisted from the very beginning of Al-Anon Family Groups that Al-Anon be a separate entity and not a subsidiary of AA.[17]

Some districts have claimed on the basis of group autonomy that dual members can serve in certain positions beyond the group level because they do not lead to membership at the World Service Conference, such as the chairperson for fundraisers, programs and other events. Some districts have also allowed dual members to serve as coordinators and newsletter editors, as well as allowed dual members to vote at the district level.

Some registered Al-Anon groups in the area appear to have only dual members as regular members. "The WSO cannot register any group that is solely for Al-Anon members who are also recovering alcoholics and members of AA, because it does not qualify to have a group representative."[18] The World Service Office has registered some groups in spite of their total dual member status, in hopes that the group would attract a non-AA member to be the group representative. Other groups are unaware of the area and World Service Conference policy and elect a dual member to a position beyond the group level. These actions have caused various problems including 1) not allowing a dual member to vote at an assembly, 2) embarrassing the dual member who is unaware of the policy and 3) disrupting a district or assembly meeting while the issue is discussed.

At the 2000 World Service Conference, a motion was discussed to change the Dual Member policy as stated in the Service Manual to show the effects of the policy only at the World Service level and to remove any reference to the policy at the area and district level from the Service Manual. That motion was defeated.

In Northern California, the motion passed by the assembly in February 1987 reads, "That the only offices or positions that can be held by a dual member are at their respective group level and would include such offices as Group Secretary, Group Treasurer, Group Literature person, etc. Further that a dual member cannot hold any position which would affect more than one group since this would indeed place that person 'above the group level,' i.e., District Coordinators, District Committee Chairmen, and like positions at the district and information service level whether they have a vote at the district or information service level or not." While some see this stand to be very harsh, the vast majority of votes at Al-Anon assemblies and the World Service Conference have repeatedly affirmed this decision.

These controversies existed and in some instances continue to exist at various times and at various levels in Al-Anon. In every case, while the controversy rages, the discussions might be heated, passionate and emotional. But after a while the controversy gets resolved to the betterment of the majority and often is adjusted to accommodate the needs of the minority.

Notes

[1] *Al-Anon Alateen Service Manual, 1998-2000*, p 92. Reprinted with permission of AFG Headquarters, Inc.

[2] *Digest of Al-Anon Policies 1983-1985*, p 42. Reprinted with permission of AFG Headquarters, Inc.

[3] *Inside Al-Anon*, Dec-Jan 1991-92, p 1. Reprinted with permission of AFG Headquarters, Inc.

[4] *Inside Al-Anon*, Aug-Sep 1989, p 2. Reprinted with permission of AFG Headquarters, Inc.

[5] The Serenity Prayer was called the AA prayer in 1941 when it was adopted by the AA fellowship. *Grateful to Have Been There*, p 87. Parkside Publishing Corporation, Park Ridge IL.

[6] Proposed at the 1974 World Service Conference and approved at the next Conference.

[7] AA introduced this statement at their 1965 International Convention.

[8] Al-Anon Family Group Headquarters, Inc publishes M-10. It includes this prayer.

[9] The motion read "That this Assembly be closed with the Serenity Prayer."

[10] This was the first motion considered by the 1991 Assembly.

[11] The motion reads, " That the closing prayer for this and future assemblies be chosen by drawing from a selection of prayers. Prayers to be included in the drawing are determined by the NCWSC (area world service committee)."

[12] *Al-Anon/Alateen Service Manual 1998-2000*, P24/P27, page 63. Reprinted with permission of Al-Anon Family Group Headquarters, Inc.

[13] Motion 8702.19 passed at the September 1987 Northern California Assembly.

[14] Pauline G. was elected to the position of Secretary of the Oakland AA Group. An early letter notes that she was not an alcoholic.

[15] *Al-Anon Family Group Forum*, June 1963, page 6. Reprinted with permission of Al-Anon Family Group Headquarters, Inc.

[16] The Dual Member policy was reaffirmed various ways in 1986, 1987, 1989, 1991, 1994, and 1996.

[17] Lois insisted on adding the sentence "Although a separate entity ..." to Tradition 6. *Lois Remembers*, p 176.

[18] *Al-Anon/Alateen Service Manual 1998-2000*, P24/P27, p 62. Reprinted with permission of Al-Anon Family Group Headquarters, Inc.

Northern California World Service Districts 1 to 27
1999

9

District, AIS, LDC, Intergroup and Council

When Al-Anon groups first organized in Northern California, their model was the organization of AA. AA had formed the Northern California Council of AA (NCCAA) in 1949. In early 1952, a note on the bulletin board of the NCCAA Conference called for the non-alcoholics to consider a meeting to form their own organization. This resulted in the formation of the Northern California Al-Anon Council, which codified their practices in a handbook around 1960. Several large cities formed their own Intergroups, including San Jose around 1963, as well as San Francisco, Oakland and Sacramento. Sometime prior to 1963, the California area assembly drew a district map, which included 19 districts for the entire state. Later on, in the mid 1970's, the World Service Office asked the Intergroups to change their name to Al-Anon Information Service (AIS) and some of the Intergroups did, including the ones in San Francisco and in Sacramento. The World Service Office then established the term, Literature Distribution Center, (LDC) to identify those Al-Anon functions that wished to purchase literature at discounted prices. This allowed these functions to create a small "profit" that allowed them to pay for other local services.

The following chapters list today's 27 districts, grouped together as the twelve districts were listed in 1964 after the state divided into two areas. Each district contributed to the chapter in some way. Some of the material was found in the NCWSA archives; others in district, Intergroup and AIS archives. Other material was found in the NCWSA newsletter, the *12 Stepper*. Several individuals also contributed their own experiences. Other organizations, like the Council, Intergroup, AIS and LDC, are mentioned as part of the district sharing. Districts have been instrumental in uniting the groups in each major city and town in Northern California. These chapters describe how each district grew. They include personal sharings about specific characteristics that may show the differences in applying the Al-Anon structure to their own circumstances.

There is no early documentation available on how the district borders were formed or how the original 19 districts were organized prior to 1963, except the map shown on page 11. After the division of California into two areas, the area divided itself into 12 districts. As presented in these chapters, the district numbers of 1964 are listed as Roman numerals I to XII. The districts divided as the number of groups grew. They began renumbering by adding a letter designation. For example, District II became District II-A and District II-B. Then in 1982, the assembly renumbered the districts and gave a blueprint for future additions. So the districts became 1 through 24 in 1982 and three additional districts were added over time.

10

Districts 1 and 2

District I prior to 1980

The first meeting in the district, the "Monday Night Eureka" group in Eureka, is about 40 years old and the newest meeting is now two months old. In the 1963 Northern California map of Al-Anon districts, district I included Del Norte, Humboldt, Mendocino and Lake counties. Sometime in the early 1980's, Mendocino and Lake counties formed their own district.

District 1

There are about 140 Al-Anon members today in district 1. Dottie J., a long time member, shares about her experiences. "At the time I joined Al-Anon in October 1974, there was one meeting in all of Humboldt County, on Monday night at 8:00 p.m. At that time, they were meeting upstairs in a small room in the Department of Motor vehicles building on 4th Street, a triangular building. There were four ladies and a small table there. The Alano Club was downstairs. Once a month the club had potlucks and Bingo. It was a great place to meet people and get to know them.

"The Monday night meeting moved to 6th and G Street. It was a little room in the back of the H & R Block Building. We still had one meeting a week. A couple of ladies were driving in from McKinleyville and Arcata. I decided to get a meeting going in Arcata. Three or four of us would drive over and help. We wanted to be there for the newcomers. Then a meeting started up in Willow Creek where they met in a church in Salyer (beside forestry). Then a meeting started in Garberville.

All the groups started as very small meetings; lots of time only the secretary showed up. Once a month we had meetings together. We named it the 'Round Robin.' We'd drive to wherever the 'host meeting' was. Each group had a different program; sometimes a video or a local speaker was part of the program.

"I complained to my sponsor that I just couldn't make it through the week on one meeting. By Thursday, I was a basket case again. She said, 'So start another meeting!' This is how the Friday night 'Study Group' began. We wanted a meeting with a different format. We based it on the Steps and Traditions and we studied our big book, *Living with an Alcoholic*[1], and some pamphlets. We only had that book, the *One Day at a Time in Al-Anon* (ODAT) and five or six pamphlets. Then the Friday afternoon meeting was born. They were trying to get the young mothers and people that didn't work out of home. It met at 2:30 PM with a babysitter. Later it was changed to a 'Brown Bag' group at noon. A Saturday night young couples group was started but didn't last long.

"When the Central Service group was formed, the officers were nominated and voted for according to our big book and service manuals. Arlene H. and I held the positions of district representative and assistant for 9 years! That's why it was 'Burn Out' for me. All the groups were so new, no one else would volunteer. We attended the NCWSA conferences. In those years they were all held in the Bay Area and in Redding, so it was an easy weekend drive. Whoever went, we shared expenses. We had no money in the treasury but we had lots of good times."

The Al-Anon groups are regularly asked to supply Al-Anon speakers at Alcoholics Anonymous events in Humboldt County. The groups have been supplying a 10-minute speaker at the AA Humboldt County Intergroup monthly speaker's meeting. In Del Norte county (Crescent City) the Al-Anon members participate on an annual basis with the Crescent City Roundup.

District 2

The first Al-Anon meeting along the Mendocino coast began in 1976 on Friday nights. The group organizers were "Skeets," Lea L. and two other women. They had been attending the AA meetings at St. Michael's church in Fort Bragg and decided that recovery depended on working on themselves. As is so typical, the AA meeting was in the church dining room, while the Al-Anon meeting was in the kitchen. Al-Anon members kept the coffee pot going for the AA members. Later, a second meeting began at the same church on Tuesday nights. Carol C. said she tried them, but "it was definitely not for me! I wasn't ready to accept that I was powerless!"

Sometime between 1983 and 1985, a Monday noon "Brown-Baggers" meeting began at the Evergreen Methodist Church in Fort Bragg. Early members were Bunny, Virginia, Loretta and Beth R. All the meetings at this time were smoking meetings, but they changed later on. Carol C. started attending this meeting and said, "It wasn't well attended, but it was always there." Carol did return to the

Friday night meeting at St. Michael's. She recently said, "These meetings were always exciting." It was well attended by old-timers and by vacationers, especially during the summer months. Once the Monday noon meeting became a non-smoking meeting, it began to grow, so the members extended it to an hour and a half.

In the early 1990's, Mary S. and her husband, Glenn S., opened the doors at the Presbyterian Church in Mendocino for a Wednesday night meeting. The early meetings were held in the schoolroom where everyone sat in the small children's chairs. The meeting grew when they moved to the choir practice room upstairs. There they sat in adult sized chairs and the windows had lace curtains. An Alateen meeting began at the same time and lasted for a couple years. When the original teens moved away and no new members joined, the meeting was dropped. It began three times like this without successfully maintaining itself. At one time, three Alateens from the Bay Area shared their stories at the Mendocino High School career day in order to build enthusiasm for a permanent Alateen meeting.

When Mary and Glenn S. moved to Mendocino from Riverside, they began attending NCWSA assemblies and NCWSC committee meetings. Prior to that time, there was little representation from District 2. They brought back information about Al-Anon in northern California and the World Service Office to the groups. This encouraged others to do likewise and now group representatives have been attending these meetings regularly. It also inspired about 10 members to attend the AA International Convention at San Diego in 1995. Two of them were speakers at the Al-Anon portion of the convention.

Other meetings in the district are the Monday night meeting at the Senior Center in Fort Bragg and a bi-weekly Monday night meeting in Sea Ranch. Lea L., who started the original Fort Bragg meeting, started a Monday night meeting in Booneville in 1999. It began with five and is now up to seven members. She recently announced, "I will not be director" and encouraged the others to take leadership roles. In order to let the townspeople know about the group, she has placed flyers in the local stores and in the town hall. There is an active meeting in Covelo, but as of now only two people are going. Covelo also has a very large Native American population. In 2000, Nancy A. from the Tuesday Ukiah meeting, spoke with Booneville group about district matters. She was attempting to set up a functioning district, encouraging those from Willits and Ukiah to join in with the coastal towns. She finished her conversation with, "I will let you know if I have any success in beginning a radio meeting."

Notes

[1] *Living With an Alcoholic*, B-5. Published by AFG Headquarters, Inc.

11

Districts 3 and 4

District II prior to 1970

In 1963 when California officially divided into two World Service areas, the district numbered district II stretched from Highway 80 north of Sacramento to the Oregon border. A map committee appointed by John F., first area chairperson, changed the borders, but they remained District II. This District II eventually became what is now Districts 3 and 4.

By 1967 the groups in Grass Valley, Chico, the Dunsmuir-Mt. Shasta Wildcats, and Redding were very active and growing. The Redding group was making an attempt to invite wives from the neighboring town of Anderson. The Marysville and Oroville groups were dormant, but getting ready to start again. A member, Sarah S., was able to help a county social worker by giving Alateen literature to her. The Paradise group was dormant, but Madeline C. was in a position to refer potential members to the Chico group.

The Twin Cities Al-Anon Family Group (Marysville/Yuba City) was registered in 1951 followed by the Chico Friday AFG in 1953, but the meetings had started in the late 1940's. Many members would "Get In The Car" to drive to nearby groups to encourage and support each other. Trips were made to Oroville, Redding and Red Bluff, Colusa, Paradise, Yuba City, Marysville, Gridley, Willows, Corning and Orland. The Corning and Willows groups are closed today.

Wives traveled with their husbands, attending Alcoholics Anonymous conferences and open meetings throughout the valley. This is the way members kept in touch with each other. When Al-Anon members attended an AA conference they would take a cake, pie or other goodies to donate to the snack bar, where other

Al-Anon members would take charge of them. This practice was dropped while the second delegate, Muriel B., was in office during 1969, because Al-Anon received no share of the profit from AA even though Al-Anon and Alateen contributed one-third of their total registration fee to Alcoholics Anonymous.

Early on, meetings were held in private homes. They began to move to churches and other facilities, with one exception. Marge A. of Chico held the Tuesday Morning Group in her home, and soon the Wednesday Night Group began, and the Sunday afternoon group met there until her death in 1994. The Sunday group still meets but in a different location. In Paradise, Madeline C. opened her home for meetings twice a month in 1963 or 1964 for a time, and then Dorothy H. began holding a meeting in her home in 1971. This meeting later moved because AA graciously agreed that the group could use a second room where they met on Thursday night.

The Northern California Council of Alcoholics Anonymous held conferences in Chico in October 1960, Marysville in 1963 and again in Chico in 1966. The Chico Friday AFG, the only meeting in town, formed the host committee to help plan part of the program. It included an Alateen Sponsor's Workshop, and a World Service meeting chaired by Ann O., NCWSA's first delegate. There were four Al-Anon speakers on Saturday afternoon, including Dorothy D. of Chico. Madeline and Bob C. of Paradise were the Sunday morning spiritual speakers. It was customary for Al-Anon members to attend AA's Saturday Night meeting, and no Al-Anon meetings were planned. Clarence S., an original member of AA, was the 1966 Saturday night speaker.

District 3

In the period from 1964 till about 1975 there were no formal district meetings. District 3, in the counties of Glenn, Butte, Plumas, Colusa, Yuba and Sierra, was the southern part of the original District II. The dividing line was between Redding and Chico. Members and newcomers were busy recovering, and learning how to keep Al-Anon and Alateen going by applying the new World Service structure within their groups. But to serve as a group representative or district committeeman was time consuming and involved travel to the metropolitan areas where most all the service meetings were held to accommodate many more members.

In 1975, Al-Anon received national publicity in Chico. The district representative from Chico reported that the author of the TV daytime series "General Hospital" lived in Chico and that author recently investigated and participated in some Al-Anon meetings in order to carry through a plot for the show about an alcoholic and how the wife sought help through Al-Anon.

Gradually, members got involved in Al-Anon service with the encouragement and information received at district meetings. Coordinators for Alateen, Public Information, Institutions and other members contacted two community colleges in Yuba and Butte counties, and Chico State College, later a University, where panels and speakers presented the Al-Anon and Alateen program. The coopera- tion of radio stations in the district was very helpful in announcing special events. Meetings on Wheels were taken to high school counselors and nursing students; an open meeting was held and a medical society was invited; radio interviews of members have taken place. Members have participated in health fairs. District meeting lists have been made available to agencies. Lorraine G., the district PI/ Institution coordinator, started an Al-Anon meeting at a health facility in Yuba City/Marysville

Alateen groups sprang up in Yuba City/Marysville, Oroville, Paradise and Quincy with the help of several enthusiastic Alateen sponsors: Pat C. of Chico, Doris M., Dottie R., Molly D., Carolyn and Liz of Yuba City, Judy B. and others from Quincy. Katie E. of Chico was the sponsor of the only Alateen group in the district today, while an Alateen group struggles in Oroville. Sponsors from Quincy, Chico and Yuba City have taken Alateens to the Northern California Alateen Con- ference. They also had an Alatot group.

In 1988 Gretchen J., the district representative, sent out a newsy letter to all the district groups, and at the following district meeting, she asked that a newslet- ter be named and started. She had previously remarked that because she had the key, she was responsible for opening the meeting that day. Teresa S. of Chico suggested we call it *THE KEY* and all agreed. Recently, the district began finan- cially supporting an annual speaker meeting to be hosted by a volunteer group. Chico groups have begun to hold a speaker meeting once a month with one of their own members. Currently the CPC/PI/Institution Coordinator, Dorothy H. of Magalia, initiated the process for members to conduct an Al-Anon meeting in a Women's Correctional facility near Yuba City. For the past five years members in the district, particularly in Marysville/Yuba City, have cooperated and participated in the planning for the Alcoholics Anonymous Sutter-Butte Round-up, held in Yuba City.

Beverley A., and Irma C. of Chico, Jackie B. and Thelma H. of Yuba City, Pat C. of Chico, La Vonne C., Yuba City, Dorothy C. of Oroville, Gretchen J. of Marysville, Sherry C. and Terry C. both of Oroville have all served as district committeemen/representatives. Irma and Jackie have served more than once. Dis- trict members began holding meetings in 1975 and decided to meet four times per year with different groups hosting it. Each meeting is different. There are meetings with speakers, workshops, raffles, white elephant sales, potluck lunches and other interesting activities. Delegates are invited to come share. District 3's current dis- trict representative is Bruce H. of Yuba City, and has already been snared to serve on the NCWSA Budget Committee. The other district trusted servants are Enid B. of Paradise, editor of the *KEY*, Dorothy H. of Magalia, PI/CPC/Institution Coordinator, Sloan D. of Oroville, Literature, Mary Ann C. of Orland, secretary, and Debbie R., Treasurer of Yuba City. Improved communication exists by e-mail today.

District 4

Al-Anon and Alateen began informal meetings in the Redding area sometime in the early 1960's. Like most Al-Anon meetings, it was mainly the wives of AA members who were accompanying their husbands to their AA meetings. As people from Southern California began moving to our cities, they brought structure and literature from their experiences with long standing meetings. They were also getting information from the Chico area members.

Locally, in 1968 a joint potluck group of AA's and Al-Anon's, Saturday Night Roving Group, was started with 40 to 50 members of both programs. Each month they held a Speaker's Meeting with an AA and/or an Al-Anon member from Southern California as speaker for the evening.

In 1971, AA members built an Alano Club giving Al-Anon a room for their meetings. This is when Al-Anon really began to grow. Until 1972 there was one AA and one Al-Anon meeting in Redding. In 1973, Faun L. was elected as our first DR. She was elected as the area delegate in 1979. Later in the 1970's and into the 1980's new meetings began to be held in churches and hospitals. District 4 includes the far northern counties of Tehama, Lassen, Shasta, Siskiyou and Modoc. As people from those outlying areas (Yreka, Mt. Shasta, Alturas, Susanville, Beiber, Burney, Weaverville, Shingletown) began to hear about Al-Anon they came long distances to attend meetings. When possible, the district representatives traveled to the outlying cities and helped them set up their own meetings. Often organizational questions and guidance took place by phone since travel on the mountain roads was dangerous and prohibitive in winter months. Older meeting lists show that there were often two and three meetings a day. As early as 1970, a core group of 15 began to hold Alateen meetings. The teens spoke at the area high schools about their experiences in dealing with alcoholics. Because of this, Alateen meetings were then started in the high schools.

Our members provided and distributed literature to public offices, drug and alcohol treatment centers, newspapers, radio and television. For instance, in the early 1980's the one local TV station did a live public service interview with Lois C., the district representative, who sat with her back to the camera answering questions about Al-Anon's purpose, functions and meetings. In 1989, the district started its own newsletter, *Stepping Power*, which is published every other month. In 1989, the district hosted the area assembly was held here in 1989 and the Summer NCWSA Conference.

In 1990 Laurie S., the district representative, shared, "We have 30 Al-Anon and Alateen meetings in a 125 mile radius." In the 1990's there were noon and evening meetings every day of the week except Sunday. The district started its first Day In Al-Anon in Shingletown. This function still takes place in Redding in the fall, offering panels and bringing in speakers from other areas. Since 1992 we have participated in the large joint AA/Al-Anon/Alateen Shasta WinterFest Conference, which is held the last weekend in January, bringing in circuit speakers from across the U. S. In 1997 we again hosted the NCWSA Assembly in Redding.

In 2000, the World Service Office lists 40 Al-Anon and Alateen meetings in our district. We held two Fun Day's at a local park. They were strictly for fun, food, games and fellowship. Some of the meetings are having Speaker Potlucks periodically. We have also added potlucks to all of our district meetings. This is more fun and encourages fellowship with people from all meetings within the entire district. We continue to visit all the more remote area meetings to give them support and encouragement to participate in district and area functions.

12

District 5

District 5 was originally called District III. The borders haven't changed since the 1964 division, and the district was renumbered District 5 in 1982. Mary B. of Santa Rosa submitted most of this sharing. For a while she also lived in San Jose. After interviewing Alateen sponsors, Richard K. and Dick P., history about the beginnings and the continuing efforts with Alateen has been added. This district has been very successful in providing Alateen in high schools and has been a model for other districts.

Mary B. shared, "In November 1962 a group of dedicated Al-Anon members decided to reactivate Al-Anon in Santa Rosa. An earlier meeting had been closed down before because it was not going at a good Al-Anon level and some wise members felt it was better not to have a meeting than to have a bad one. As time went on, they began to see more new people attending AA meetings with their spouses, so they decided to try again. I feel it was started for me since I am the only one still attending meetings of the people who were there back then.

"The meeting was held Saturday night at the Congregational church on the corner of Humboldt and Silva where there was one of the few AA meetings in Santa Rosa. About two years later (1964) some of us decided we could use more meetings and we started a Wednesday night meeting at 70 South East Street at the old Alano Club. (Our old, green Alano Club has long since been torn down.) Some of the older members thought the new meeting would detract from the Saturday night meeting, but we all promised to attend both meetings. Since we were well aware of keeping it at a good level of Al-Anon, we went ahead with the meeting and it worked very well.

"We tried to start meetings in smaller towns (Petaluma, Sebastopol, Healdsburg), but in those days, spouses were afraid that everyone in their town would find out that their spouses had a drinking problem, so they would rather go to meetings in Santa Rosa. Additionally, at that time there were only couples looking for meetings; mothers, fathers, children and friends of alcoholics eventually came, all looking for help in dealing with the person in their lives with a drinking problem.

"We had no group representatives in those days, but couples would go to conferences and bring back the information we needed to keep us informed about Al-Anon business administration. As other meetings started we would have an information meeting once a month where the secretaries would meet to help each other with suggestions on how to cope with problems in their home meetings. These suggestions usually came from the guidelines, the 12 Steps and 12 Traditions. Occasionally we wrote to World Service for help. We were determined to keep on track and not get into other therapies or hold gripe and gossip sessions.

"We started Alateen about three years after we had Al-Anon going pretty well, and we took turns sponsoring. We had to go through growing pains with trying to have sponsors that had their Al-Anon programs going well. We were not there to rescue the Alateen members, but we were there to give them the tools of the program to help them cope so they could make better decisions in their lives. There are three full time meetings, one at the Hanna Boys Center and two in Santa Rosa. The Friday night meeting at the Church of Roses meets at the same time as the AA, Al-Anon and a Pre-Alateen meeting."

About 1991, Dick P. of Geyserville started several Alateen meetings in the Santa Rosa and Healdsburg schools. He said, "We have found it best to share that we come together as a family. In Alateen, we learn to care, not only for ourselves, but for our family members as well. We practice fraternal love within the meeting. Criticism of our family does not enhance recovery." There are two meetings at each school, with Santa Rosa meeting on Tuesdays and the Healdsburg meeting on Friday. The teens can choose which meeting they attend, so that they don't always miss the same school period. The meetings have no restrictions imposed on them by the school. New Alateen members hear of the meeting from counselors or through other students by word-of-mouth. Towards the end of the year, the seniors speak to classes about Alateen. At this point, they are less concerned about their own anonymity. Dick also shares at school functions and includes the video *Alateen Tells it Like It Is*[1] as part of his presentation.

The district selects co-sponsors for the group. They hold monthly sponsors' workshops. When a person regularly attends these workshops, it is a sign that they are willing to serve as a sponsor. Individuals are recruited at meetings and other district functions. Once they express an interest, they also come to the Alateen meeting as a speaker. There is a clearance sheet[2] the potential sponsor is required to sign. The sponsors of the school meetings take the job of sponsor seriously. They encourage the teens to remain on topic, not to speak out of turn and to assure that gossip and roughhousing are not allowed. Dick said, "This is especially important for a school meeting. We need to be sure that the school sees the Alateen meeting as profitable for the school."

We were very involved with the conferences held here in Santa Rosa. We took care of the meetings, speakers, registration, as well as furnishing our share of cookies for the common gathering room for coffee and goodies. Lots of good armchair-sharing going on as families attended each other's meetings. We were doing the sixth Tradition.

In District 5 we now have approximately thirty-eight Al-Anon, nine Alateen and two Pre-Alateen meetings, group representatives, and a monthly district meeting."

Notes

[1] *Alateen Tells It Like It Is*, AV-16, is available from Al-Anon Family Group Headquarters, Inc.

[2] This clearance sheet requires that the person declare that they have not been accused of sexual abuse and other items. This is done to protect the teens and the sponsors.

13

Districts 6, 7, 8, 9, 10 and Sacramento AIS/LDC

The Early Days

The first Alcoholics Anonymous group in the Sacramento area was described in a letter written to the Secretary of the Alcoholic Foundation in New York. This letter informed the Foundation that their second AA meeting occurred the previous night and that they had eight members.

George S.[1] from Loomis recounted how he and his wife first found AA in 1949. "I worked nights. After she put our two children to bed, my wife watched programs like Milton Berle's Texaco Theater on our new Hoffman television and drank. One day as she was looking through the *Auburn Journal*, she saw an ad. It said, 'If you have a problem or have a friend who has a problem with drinking, call this number' and she did.

"They told her someone would come to call on her the next evening. But she didn't tell me. Two mornings later, when I got up to make breakfast for the children and clean up a bit, I noticed an ashtray had cigarette butts in them. Neither of us smoked. The boys mentioned that Mamma had some visitors the night before; a lady and a man came and they smoked. Alice B. and Floyd B. had come up from Roseville and had made a 12th Step call on her. Alice came back that night to take her to the Tuesday Night Roseville AA meeting and continued to do so until I could change my work schedule. In those early days of AA most of the meetings were open meetings. The friend or spouse of an alcoholic could attend but not participate. We made ourselves useful by making coffee, serving donuts and coffee, emptying ashtrays and talking to each other."

In November 1949, a non-alcoholic group called the Nalano Group was formed
in Sacramento, where Floyd G. was the first secretary. The Mother Group is probably this group. George reflects on various names proposed for groups. "When we
were around an AA meeting and not a member, we were referred to as a 'non-
alcoholic', or 'friends of AA' or 'spouses of AA'. In early 1951, the AA Central
Office in New York was receiving many letters from groups, friends and spouses of
alcoholics from around the country. One of the names that came up was 'Souses'
Spouses,' but they didn't think this would go over very well."

In early 1953, Lois W. drafted a letter to both the AA delegates and the Al-
Anon groups. The Clearing House asked the groups whether they would accept
the Traditions as presented. The number of groups who responded was low. But
four groups from Northern California, including the Sacramento Group[2], answered
the letter.

George moved away from Sacramento in 1952 for five years and lived in San
Jose. When he returned, the groups were organized. A governing board[3] was elected
for three years, including a chairman, secretary and treasurer. At this time, representatives of districts IV[4] through X would come to a council meeting every other
month with ideas. In 1964 the boundaries of district II were changed so that those
groups in Auburn and Grass Valley could attend district meetings in Sacramento,
which was easier for them rather than going to the north towards Chico. Sadi C.
recalls there was a "Family Afterwards" meeting in Fair Oaks in the 1960's. This
meeting was for both AA and Al-Anon members. George S. remembers that hugging was common in the early days. Irma C. of Chico remembers that members
put an arm around the shoulder in the late 1960's; Bob J. remembers in the 1970's
that he avoided those who hugged. All agreed that hugging is common today, but
that we usually ask first.

Rapid growth generates more service

In September1970, the groups hired a telephone answering service. That month
they received 83 phone calls, for a monthly cost of $19.00. Groups made monthly
contributions of mostly $3.00 to $5.00 to pay for the service, though some contributed a little less and some contributed a bit more. Pamphlets were mailed to
the callers. Most of the literature sent out is still on the tables of Al-Anon, but one
stands out, *How an AA Wife Lives the 12 Steps*[5]. In 1971, there was a dinner to
honor those who volunteered for TeleService. The dinner was paid from the sale of
a cake and a raffle, which grossed $79.55 and the event netted $54.51. In June of
1992, the Tele-Service received 515 calls. Sixteen volunteers were thanked for their
time devoted to volunteering at the AIS office.

In 1972, the WSO sent a letter to Norma who was listed as the permanent
mailing address for the AIS, notifying her that she would receive a free copy of the
monthly *FORUM* and occasional other materials to share with the group. In October 1972, Flo B., who started the Sacramento Tele-Service died. A tribute to her

said in part, "Without her Al-Anon would still be on the shirt tails of AA. Her Higher Power will give her a diploma 'summa cum laude'".

In December 1973, the AIS published its first newsletter and shortly after, it was named the *Share and Care*. It warns those who want to contribute. "To keep resentments at an all-time low, the news must be in writing to avoid any mistakes in wording." It also announced the upcoming election of officers of the AIS in January. They announced the first Public Speaker meeting sponsored by the Al-Anon Information Service. At this meeting, a skit was presented in the form of a TV interview, with Dick C. as the television host and Vera C. impersonating "Mom's Mobley". "You all come ... 'Mom's' was in Concord last month and they gave her a standing ovation."

Amber E. purchased literature from the WSO and stored the books in her Datsun halfback. Amber was the first person in Sacramento to purchase the ODAT in sufficient quantities to get a $0.50 per book discount. In 1978, Earthel N. started the literature depot in her home. This continued for 10 years. Many of her orders were shipped by mail. Other volunteers, including Idell and Catherine, would come to Earthel's home to help out. She converted one of her four bedrooms into an office and storage for the literature center. They not only mailed literature to groups locally, but to cities like Stockton, Napa, Fairfield and Nevada City. When the AIS took over literature sales in 1987, she had a total profit of $22,000 to give to the AIS as their beginning funds.

Bob J. describes the need for individuals to serve. "Today in district 7 only four group representatives from 14 groups attend the business meeting, and there is no one who has volunteered to become the alternate district representative." Max V. suggests that it is OK for old-timers like him to "volunteer" some others into service. Bob J. wrote a letter about service to members, which is published in the September 2000 issue of the *Share and Care*.

Some groups and their activities

In 1964, the World Service Office Directory listed meetings in Davis, Fairfield (The Twin City Al-Anon), Vallejo, Woodland, North Sacramento, Citrus Heights, Lodi, four in Sacramento (South Sacramento, Thursday Night, Nalano and North), Nevada City (Gold Quartz) and Placerville (Hangtown).

The meetings listed in the December 1973 newsletter are different from the earlier ones: Mother Group, Midway Point Group, New meetings: Camino Monday Nite Group (8 miles north of Placerville), Broderick/Brite Group, Tahoe City Thursday Night Group, Elk Grove meeting (Catholic church on Parkway), and two with address changes: Alano North Alateen (Carmichael) and Folsom Al-Anon (Presbyterian Church).

A Men's Stag meeting started in March 1974, but it later disbanded. Bob J. formed a new Stag meeting, the Thursday Night Men's Al-Anon Group. "On a

Sunday evening in early July at the Roseville meeting, the secretary asked if there were any Al-Anon announcements. I raised my hand up and said, 'There will be a new men's meeting starting very soon.' Asked when and where it would be, I thought real quickly about what was a 'bad TV night,' and said, 'Thursday and I'm not sure of the location yet.' To this day I truly believe my Higher Power took control, because the announcement came as a surprise—even to me. That was the start of one of the oldest continuing men's groups in the country. With my Higher Power still in tight control I went to the Mercy San Juan Hospital where we were given a meeting room on Thursdays (the only night there was an available room)."

When Bob first broached the subject of a Men's meeting, he received several critical phone calls from women. The concerns were that the group would be a special focus and "not for everyone." After it started, the criticism faded. Max V. would jokingly tell women who wanted to crash the meeting, "If you can wear a tux and look like a man, you can come."

The first meeting was on July 17, 1977 and for the first 12 years the meeting was "open ended" with many of them lasting until almost midnight. "The first night, seven men attended the meeting, and that was really surprising because there were only three men who attended Al-Anon meetings regularly in the area at that time. The word spread rapidly, and within about a month, an average of 12-15 men met. The group moved into a much larger meeting room after about 5 years as we were now averaging 50 to 65 men at every meeting. We met at the hospital until the mid 1980's and had to move due to a change in hospital policy. We moved to a church a few miles away into much smaller facilities and the meeting dropped in size to about 15-20 men. After a few years at the church, we moved to our present location and today we average 20-30 per meeting. Through the years we have had perhaps as many as a thousand different men attend and we still have a core group of 'old timers' that attend almost every week. We also have many members of AA attend on a regular basis. It is very common to hear statements like, 'I sure am glad there is a men's meeting, I feel I can share and bond here.' I'm very proud of the fact the group has never missed meeting on Thursday night, even when it fell on days like Thanksgiving, Christmas Eve or New Years Eve. Also, two other men's groups have spun off this group here in the Sacramento area through the years. I have heard that many of the female Al-Anon members request that their male friends and relatives attend this meeting. We held a 10th Anniversary Open Meeting with about 300 attending the Pot Luck/Bar-B-Que. The late Ray C. from San Jose was our guest speaker. Plans are now being made to celebrate our 25th Anniversary with another big open meeting and party."

George S. said in a 1993 sharing, "In November 1974, the Mother Group celebrated its 27th anniversary." (Since this group was actually formed around 1948 or 1949, the anniversary date was probably a bit incorrect.) The Mother Group is still meeting in district 7. But it has a new name: "Monday Night El Camino Ave. AFG", which meets at the North Sacramento United Methodist Church 650 El Camino Ave, Sacramento. Margaret H. remembers when the Women's group, now meeting at Kaiser hospital, met at a beauty parlor. The Brown Bagger's group meets at noon, and workers bring their lunch. Margaret H. noticed one man who brought a brown bag, but didn't open it or eat anything during the meeting. When she asked him he said he thought he had to show up with a brown bag. He had his cookie to eat during his afternoon break at work. There was a Gay group who met on Riverside Blvd. The building that housed their original location burned down.

The 2000 meeting schedule lists 140 meetings, of which eleven are Alateen, two are Alatot, eight are adult child, five Spanish, four men, one women, one parents, and one gay meeting. Ten of the meetings don't allow children while seven provide babysitting, and there are three smoking meetings.

Districts 6 though 10

In October 1978, district IV was divided into five districts and numbered 4A (Vallejo, Travis, Davis, Woodland and Winters), 4B (Sacramento north of the American River), 4C (Sacramento south of the American River), 4D (Folsom, Lake Tahoe, Pine Grove) and 4E (Roseville, Auburn, Grass Valley, Nevada City). In 1982, when the area renumbered all the districts, these became districts 6, 7, 8, 9 and 10. Margaret H. didn't like the split of D-IV into five, because they were lettered 4-A through 4-E. She was grateful when the area renumbered the districts into 6 though 10 in 1982.

The Al-Anon Information Service Office

The first AIS officers were elected in January 1974. There was also a contest to name the newsletter. By April the newsletter found a name, *Share and Care*, and continues to be published today.

The AIS representatives elected Max V. as the chairman of AIS in 1976. Though he had expressed his willingness to some people, he was surprised that he was nominated and elected while absent and working a swing shift. The following year he was re-elected. Max and Earthel N. came into Al-Anon the same month in the previous year, February 1975.

In September 1987 a group of Al-Anon members decided there was a need to open a central information office. The first location, for three years, was at 3625 Marconi. When the lease was up, they moved to 4343 Marconi. The office assumed the responsibility for storing and selling literature and for answering the help line. Today they are located at 5429 Palm Avenue.

Public Information was quite active. There were meetings at the Sacramento County jail, Vacaville State prison, and women's shelters. In 1982, when Earthel N. was district representative, they started an Alateen meeting in the juvenile center at Kieffer Blvd. Margaret H. purchased sets of books and Chuck M., who was a traveling salesman, put them in libraries and treatment hospitals throughout the districts. They attended health fairs, mostly at colleges and in malls. Bob J. described one person, a Middle-Eastern woman (at least in dress) who walked by the Al-Anon booth three times. He finally asked if he could help. She took every pamphlet available, but never said a word. Artha O. made a game for use at the health fairs to attract participants to the booth and the game was very successful in doing so.

Counselors often sent clients to Al-Anon, sometimes requiring them to get cards signed. Margaret H. learned to sign the cards only after the meeting after one person left immediately after she signed the card.

Speaker Meetings

Eileen J. started a speaker's meeting in 1988 while she was the district representative of District 7. This meeting continues today. The district has a speaker coordinator. Speakers are mostly local, but sometimes a speaker is invited from the area. Marilyn R., the current area delegate, spoke at their November, 2000 meeting. They have had both AA and Al-Anon speakers. After a while the meeting expanded to include a potluck dinner. In 2000, they began experimenting with just dessert and coffee instead of a potluck dinner.

District 10 has had a speakers meeting during the same period. They usually have two short 10-minute speakers and followed by a 30-minute speaker. The short speakers were often Al-Anon members who hadn't spoken before—this was a training ground for them. Margaret H. has held two annual potlucks at her home for 25 years. These began as a monthly potluck that rotated between members' homes. She ended up with March and October, which continues today. At her last one, the 35 people attending had 675 years in the program.

Notes

[1] Based on interview of George S. on April 3, 1993.

[2] The Sacramento group responded on 4 April 1953. *First Steps*, p 83.

[3] The governing board was the Northern California Al-Anon Council and is described in Chapter 2.

[4] These districts are seen on the 1963 map of California on page 11.

[5] *How an AA Wife Lives the 12 Steps* was originally an article printed in August 1953 issues of *AA Grapevine*. The material in the pamphlet was included as part of *Lois' Story*, P-11, printed in 1971. In 1995, P-11 was printed in *How Al-Anon Works for Families & Friends of Alcoholics* (B-22), pages 135-142. The pamphlet itself was discontinued in 1995.

14

District 11

In 1964, this district was known as District V. It was renumbered District 11 in 1982.

As noted in *First Steps,* Vivienne F. from San Rafael notified the Clearing House that in 1952, the Northern California Council of Al-Anon had formed at a Northern California AA Council Conference in San Rafael. By 1953 the Al-Anon Council had a 2-day session in Vallejo with a "fine program." Regrettably, we have not been successful in reaching any Al-Anon members of that era. We do know, however, that the earliest group of record known to us was held at the First Presbyterian Church of San Rafael and was active in 1959. One of our current members attended that group.

In the late sixties, the group divided into several others, including two Al-Anon groups held at the Redwoods Presbyterian Church in Larkspur, the Friday Morning and the Tuesday 12: 30 P.M. Today, both of these groups continue to attract a good number of members on a regular basis. And, needless to say, the "law of supply and demand" played a role in extending our meeting roster by several more meetings.

By 1978 there were ten Al-Anon and two Alateen groups in Marin County. Ten years later, our meeting roster exploded from ten registered Al-Anon groups to thirty-eight, along with three Alateen groups, one of which had both a preteen meeting and a regular Alateen meeting.

In the 80's our district included a number of Al-Anon Adult Children of Alcoholics groups that attracted huge membership. In the year 2000 there are a total of 26 groups, including two Al-Anon Adult Children groups, one group for beginners, one for men, three for women, one for the Spanish speaking, one for parents, two for Alateen and one for Preteen Alateen. Three groups study the Steps, one studies the *Paths To Recovery* book, and ten are regular topic meetings. It is interesting to note that the membership of every Al-Anon group includes a significant percentage of adult children of alcoholics, as well as dual members.

The service structure included the traditional district meeting and an Intergroup (Information Service) meeting. In later years, the two service arms combined. Group representatives, led by the district representative, now meet once a month to discuss district matters and also perform the services of an information service as defined by the World Service Handbook.

Most groups in the district are in a position to offer financial support to the projects of the district. The main fundraiser historically has been an annual event held in late September or early October. This event started out as a sit-down dinner for 100 people. After six years, this event became so popular that the format changed to a potluck dinner in order to accommodate all who cared to attend. In the year 2000, we will have had 23 such annual events.

District 11 usually celebrates Al-Anon's birthday, May 1951, by planning A Day in Al-Anon in the month of May. This is designed to be a celebration of our program, not a fundraiser, and has always proved to be a day of fellowship that is quite popular and well attended.

In 1964, after the California area was divided into two, the district boundaries included Larkspur, Mill Valley, Novato and San Rafael. At the time it was numbered District V. After the 1982 area assembly, the districts were renumbered and this district became District 11. This is one of the districts that didn't change its boundaries as it grew.

District 11 hosted the 1983 NCWSA Assembly at the Holiday Inn in San Rafael.

In her 1993 report to the assembly, Linda J. reported, "It has been a good year for us. We had a wonderful potluck dinner last November. The potluck raises funds to operate our telephone service. Our district and Intergroup now meets together on the fourth Tuesday of each month. 15 to 20 coordinators attend. This year we have been faced with some difficult problems with not very easy answers. I am proud of the group representatives who worked hard at finding solutions. We have a literature distribution center which opens one-half hour prior to the combined district/Intergroup meeting. Most of the groups send representatives to purchase literature. There is a workshop for Alateen sponsors and those have an interest in Alateen each month. An Alateen meeting began in one of our high schools. Then the school closed. We hope to try again at another school."

Cordie T. reported in 1996 that there were 26 meetings in Marin County, including one Alateen meeting. In May the district had a Day In Al-Anon, sponsored by a group that disbanded. The district is grateful for their service as they celebrated Al-Anon's 45th anniversary. This, the second year of using a voice mail system has saved "tons of money" with no complaints. Six of our groups attended the area's special assembly. Two of the group representatives shared how excited they were to study the Traditions and Concepts. The situation leading to the special assembly was painful for the area. If this inspired members to study our legacies, it has not been in vain. Our area delegate, Art B., came to our August meeting, taking Cathy C. and Marilyn R. with him. He gave us a report all three years of his term and continues to be gracious and helpful. At their Potluck donation drawing this year, the first prize is one week's lodging in a three-bedroom condo on Maui, airfare not included.

Galey S. reported in 1999 that there are 27 meetings including Alateen and Preteen meetings. Prateeksha did a wonderful workshop on the preteen program, attended by 19 members. The district is proud of the work done for our Alateen members, including getting into the schools. Susan R. and her committee of seven did a bang-up job with Public Outreach, concentrating on getting the word into institutions.

15

Districts 12, 13 and 25

Early Groups and Events in D-VI

District 12 is the home of the first non-alcoholic group in Northern California. Much has been written of their contributions in Chapter 1. This meeting opened its doors in September 1945. The Mission Al-Anon Group is the oldest meeting still in existence. It began in 1961. Originally it met at the Salvation Army building on 3550 Army Street. Today it meets in a new location on Alemany. Other early meetings were the Grupo Latina de Al-Anon, which met on 7th Avenue, the Ocean Al-Anon group, the Sunset Al-Anon group, which still meets at 39th and Lawton, and Westlake Al-Anon. There was a panel that met the 2nd Wednesday of each month at Laguna Honda hospital.

Before 1963, the boundaries of the district, which was then labeled District 5, included the area from San Francisco on the north to Palo Alto in the south. In 1963, after the World Service Conference approved the division of California into two areas, the districts were renumbered. This district became District VI. Then in 1982, the San Francisco district became District 12. The Intergroup performed all service and fellowship/social functions. This service body followed the World Service Intergroup Guidelines. Intergroup officers and representatives were elected annually.

During the 1960's, the Al-Anon Intergroup had a desk at the San Francisco Alcoholics Anonymous Office, located downtown at 166 Geary Blvd, Room 129. That office was closed in 1970 because AA, who shared their office with us, moved. Their new location was either not considered convenient for us or became too expensive. A telephone answering service was hired to take phone numbers of newcomers. Members from groups called the service for the newcomers' numbers and returned calls and/or send literature or meeting lists. There were regular problems with this over the years, for example, calls not being picked up and calls being forwarded that cost the district more money.

A member volunteered to house the literature and fill the orders for the Intergroup. In 1975, we received an average of two letters a day and we sent out three packets of information daily. Because of the enormity of this service position, the rotation of this job was very difficult. One volunteer did this service for 4 years and the next for five years.

In August 1972, the Intergroup meetings moved out of people's homes and began meeting at the War Memorial Building in Daly City. Minutes of these meetings had a notation about the treasurer being paid "dues". On November 1970, the treasurer's report listed a balance of $140.63. The two earliest Intergroup representatives were Dolores M. and Ruth M. Two of the earliest Alateen sponsors mentioned are Lynn and Dolores M. Over the years more structure developed. An excerpt from November 1971 reads: "It is suggested we keep the meeting to one hour. Interjections by raising of hand only. 2 minutes if possible for each person."

During the 1960's and 1970's, special meetings often invited outside speakers, generally priests or doctors. Some of the speakers were Father Gerhart, Dr. Gil, Fr. Joe Martin, Dr. O'Brien, Dr. Earl, Duffy, Fr. Tom and Father "Jake". It's important to remember that during this period little was still understood about the family disease of alcoholism so professionals offered validation to us. Occasionally, meetings had a slide presentation or a movie about alcoholism. There was a great deal of use of circuit speakers including Elsa C. and Chuck C. from Laguna Beach, CA, Yvonne from Pittsburg, Blanche D. from Odessa, TX, Ramona from Oklahoma and Estelle and Harvey E. from Woodland. A long-timer tells a story about hearing Estelle speak and telling Ellen T. how impressed she was. Ellen suggested asking Estelle for her phone number. When asked, Estelle gave her number in her typical manner–in a gelatin capsule. It was common to have retreats announced during meetings. During that same period, fellowship was nurtured through potlucks as fundraisers several times a year. They would typically have an AA, Al-Anon and Alateen speaker. A 1971 potluck discussion notes "Aluminum pie tins are needed for ashtrays. Bring one can of food for raffle." During the 1970s, we usually had a Fall Luncheon and a Holiday Function. These fundraisers kept the district supplied with literature for their services. A publication called *Wife of the Alcoholic*[1], the chapter to the wives out of the *Alcoholics Anonymous* and *Search for Serenity* were discussed. "These were not conference approved but we will continue to order and ask New York why they are not" was noted in the San Francisco archives.

It was during the 1970's that Al-Anon reached out to the community for educational purposes. We spoke at schools, both high schools and universities. We had more contact with the media and even the police department contacted us for information. We placed a table at conventions, particularly those of a medical or mental health nature. We even gave literature to local businesses including AAA and Bank of America. We placed announcements in an AA newsletter called *Good News*.

Several groups reported their status at the Intergroup: Mission, "ok, has new members"; Sunset, "not as large, but has new members"; Ocean, "okay, working on better (diversified) organization"; San Bruno (Thurs) "lacks continuity, getting away from Al-Anon"; Pacific Heights-Marina "needs help!"; San Mateo "needs organization"; Hope, "needs more group participation"; 19th Ave, "needs more general participation"; Westlake, "problems are straightening out (had a steering committee)"; Letterman, "fine, AA meeting next door"; Richmond, "sick, stagnant, needs new blood & ideas"; "Alateens have picked up." From those same minutes came a discussion about San Francisco and San Mateo having a separate answering service and Intergroup, but did nothing. Earlier in the minutes "Mary suggested starting a stag group – ask men about idea and find a group leader." A group was formed immediately thereafter.

July 1973 minutes have several remarkable entries: "$10 was agreed on for the Intergroup donation (tri-annual) to New York World Headquarters." "The newly announced Saturday evening combination AA and Al-Anon group in the Methodist Church on Southgate in Westlake is disbanded. It will be AA only." "Ruth M. will negotiate with babysitter at the Ocean group. Last week the Ocean group had 22 children needing a sitter." "Grupo Geneva is having a breakdown in morale as the result of gossip within the group. It was suggested a steering committee be formed to approach the offender and explain the damage she is doing."

In 1974, the mention of a group representative was a first in the minutes. "Charlotte reminded us that we should have a group representative for World Service. Each group should try to find 1 stable person in the group whom they think will be with the group for a while." Out of 15 meetings reporting their membership, 6 had 15 or fewer attendees, 9 had 15 to 30 attendees and of those 9, 6 had between 20 and 30 attendees. In May the district changed its name to San Francisco Al-Anon Information Services. In December, Reverend Joseph Kellerman, author of *Alcoholism, A Merry-Go-Round Named Denial*[2] came to San Francisco and spoke to a full house of over 1000 people at St Mary's Cathedral. 25 members attended the March Intergroup meeting. In August 1977, the topic of gossip in meetings, a recurring problem, was addressed. It was suggested that the "3 Deadly Enemies"[3] be referred to. Redwood City decided to create their own literature center, because it was inconvenient to go to the literature person's home in San Francisco. At the September meeting there is a reference to problems, "Non-Al-Anon practices were discussed and it was agreed that procedures such as the 'hot seat' and applying pressure to Al-Anon and Alateen members was unacceptable and dangerous."

In 1978, the ABC TV station, Channel 7 showed the Alateen movie, *Francesca, Baby* and in February, the radio stations KYUU and KNBR aired a panel discussion about living with an alcoholic after Sobriety. Terry of San Francisco was the Alateen speaker. Mary's Help Hospital (now Seton Medical Center) announced the showing of a brand new film by Father Joseph Martin entitled *Alcoholism and the Family*. Al-Anon sent two or three representatives to participate on a panel.

Near the end of her term as district representative, it became evident to Lois B. that the representatives from the southern part of the district were having trouble attending the business meetings. Many felt that it was time to divide the district. Group representatives from the entire district met at Breuner's Community room to make these decisions. Two districts were formed; District 6A was from San Francisco through Millbrae; District 6B was from Burlingame through Palo Alto. Funds were provided to District 6B to establish their own literature depot.

Sharing from D -12

Joan M., the new District 6A representative, and Bev M. from District 6B, presented the two districts to the assembly in February 1979 and the assembly approved. During Joan's term, the district began functioning. Intergroup was renamed Information Service as suggested by revised World Service guidelines. Duplication of effort was identified by both service organizations. They worked together deciding that Information Services would handle the business of Literature, Teleservice and fellowship events. District handled the business of Alateen, Institutions and Public Information. Since attendance at the Information Service meeting dropped, the district and Information Service held joint meetings.

The WSO announced that the publication *The Forum* would no longer be free. It was also in October 1978 that Hank G., Trustee and Chairman of Public Information at AFG Headquarters in NY, spoke at the Mission Al-Anon meeting. Starting in 1978 and continuing into 1979, District 12 teamed with surrounding areas, Marin and San Jose to pay for TV spots for Al-Anon. In the May 1979 minutes there is a notation "Alateens are feeling neglected. They need support," and, "Intergroup funds are low." The letter, which was a thank you for the "adventure" of the previous year and for "sharing your love and support" also addressed the drop in treasury funds as a result of redistricting and splitting of funds, leaving the district with a balance of $900.

In August 1979, a man in the fellowship who did not have children introduced a phrase at Intergroup regarding Alateen. This phrase was created to remind Al-Anons about Alateen and was adopted by several Al-Anon groups in the district. It reads, "Alcoholism is a family disease. We would like to remind you that our children are also affected and that there is a program of support and help for them called Alateen." Cathy C. was later a part of the committee which brought the phrase to the area, adding the words "ages 12 to 20" to the end of the statement.

In 1980, a "phone service committee" was formed in an effort to address the ongoing phone service problems. From this arose a service position of phone chairperson to help organize this service. In March, the District 6A Newsletter was born. It has continued throughout the years since with a revision of name. They agreed to send our newsletter to all the districts in California and to mail one copy of the newsletter to groups not represented at Intergroup Meeting. In August, the newsletter introduced cartoons produced by a local member. One cartoon has an Al-Anon group sitting around a table and one member says, "For our group purpose there is but one authority…any nominations?"

The San Francisco Intergroup voted to raise the necessary funds to open a Central Office. They decided that they would restructure as a district rather than Intergroup, with Intergroup being the communication arm of the district. In June they decided that all group donations would filter through the district and that 35% will go to the district and 65% went to Intergroup.

In February 1982, the district number changed from 6A to District 12. In March the newsletter changed its name to *District 12 Newsletter*. In 1983, during Steve F.'s term, the district meetings moved to the San Francisco French Hospital. The district voted to establish an office at 102 Oak Street, San Francisco. This centralized the literature depot, Teleservice and the Public Information requests for speakers. Near the end of Steve's term, it again became evident at district meetings that the representatives from the southern part of the district were having trouble supporting the business meetings. Two districts were formed; District 12 included the City of San Francisco and one meeting in Daly City. District 25 included Daly City through Burlingame. Funds and literature were split between the two districts.

Some fundraisers for the Central Office included dances, raffles, Round Robin meetings, cloth book covers, and a pancake breakfast. Although we had monthly fundraisers, in July they announced that contributions were not up enough to support an office. Annual district events began donating their profits to fund the Central Office. That month 28 members attended the Intergroup meeting.

In November a new column "Principles in Al-Anon" appeared in the newsletter. In December a column featuring personal shares on the Traditions began and other personal stories of recovery were requested. A reminder also appeared, "that if you are a member of the Adult Children of Alcoholics Al-Anon group please do not refer to the group as ACA. This request was made because there is a non Al-Anon meeting known as Adult Children of Alcoholics and we do not want to be confused with them as they too go by the initials ACA."

In January 1983, the Central Office Fund Raising Committee reached its funding goal and the proceeds were turned over to Intergroup for the planning phase. Also in January, the district received a letter from the "Saturday Night Literature AFG" asking Al-Anon to consider changing or eliminating male pronouns in the steps. In March, "Joan suggested that the group consider adopting the name 'Information Services' versus using Intergroup. At the April Intergroup meeting there were 60 groups in District 12. In July a Poster Drive was a great success!! Approximately 150 Al-Anon/Alateen Posters were placed throughout District 12, in such places as ethnic community bulletin boards, medical offices, laundromats, and stores frequented by teens. The Professional's Luncheon was also successful. 72 persons attended, about one-half were professionals from a wide range of social positions, including judges, nurses, ministers, recovery counselors, and recreational and business personnel. In September, redistricting was taken to the assembly and approved. In October our Central Office was opened and named the Information Service Office."

In 1984, a member submitted an article about discovering the Twelve Concepts: "I've always had a sneaking suspicion that someplace there had to be a book of Al-Anon rules, and I was sure I'd just found it. How embarrassing to read the first Concept, and find that whoever was at the top refused to take the power, but passed it back to the groups."

Seven Spanish-speaking Al-Anon groups of the San Francisco Bay Area participated in the 12th Annual National Spanish-speaking AA Convention held August 31, September 1 and 2. It was a big plus for Al-Anon attraction for the local Spanish-speaking Al-Anon members, who also felt the warmth of the fellowship as some members participated from as far away as Canada and Puerto Rico.

In 1985, our newsletter was renamed *Reaching Out*. The January newsletter introduced a recovery musical called "Beach Blanket Al-Anon". It was described as "a musical sharing of our lives, and a buoyant celebration of our strengths and victories." A quote in that newsletter reads: "In recovery, we sometimes find ourselves where we would rather not be before we can get where we need to be." An article in the May edition of the newsletter was entitled "In Touch with Alateen". A personal share from Jackie, our Alateen Coordinator, is a plea that reads in part "Have you noticed the growth in Al-Anon meetings in San Francisco these days? Most obvious, is the increasing numbers of Adult Children meetings! There are now seven meetings. Al-Anon is gaining strength as people realize the effect alcoholism has had in their lives, but Alateen is not. These meetings are few and have little and diminishing attendance. There is an increasing knowledge and acceptance that young people are seriously affected by alcoholism in their families. Years that should be happy, carefree and constructive become years of nightmares, bitterness and discouragement. I lived with the disease and didn't realize the effect it had on my life until after I came into Al-Anon. I was 31 before I let 'help' intervene in my life." In July, the district dropped the *Reaching Out* title for the newsletter and returned to its earlier name, *District 12 Newsletter*, Vol. 9 No. 7. District 12 and 25 held a joint picnic in Stern Grove on Sunday, August 31st. The Intergroup meetings have finally been integrated into the district meeting. In 1987, the newsletter printed its first article in Spanish and in December, its first sharing from an Alateen member. In 1988, the district formed a softball league and incorporated as a non-profit corporation.

District 13

Prior to 1979, this district was part of District VI. After the division, this district formed what was the southern part of District VI and now covers the mid-peninsula from Burlingame south to and including Palo Alto and from East Palo Alto to Half Moon Bay on the coast.

David B., treasurer of District 13 in 1985, shared his experiences with obtaining non-profit status for the district. "I recognized that nonprofit status for the organization would be beneficial. We could get bank services without any fees, as I recall, and donors to the organization would be entitled to claim their contributions as tax deductions. The District 13 business meeting endorsed the idea. At first I pursued nonprofit status as an unincorporated organization. A committee developed the bylaws. The consensus of the committee, and eventually the business meeting, was that we should incorporate before seeking nonprofit status. We filed the papers with the California Secretary of State on May 1, 1985. On November 18th we filed for tax-exempt status with the IRS. On December 24, 1985, the IRS requested additional information and one or more minor changes in our articles of incorporation. These were submitted to the IRS on January 25, 1986, and the IRS responded by granting tax-exempt status, 501(c)(3), on February 24, 1986. The minor changes to the articles that had been requested by the IRS meant that we had to submit the changes to the Secretary of State as well. These were submitted on January 31, 1986, as an amendment to the articles of incorporation. The incorporation and nonprofit status apply to the District 13 Al-Anon Information Service only, not to Al-Anon groups within District 13."

In 1990, the district had 46 meetings, including eight Adult Child, four Alateen, two Gay/Lesbian, two Spanish and one Parent's meeting. The district moved its literature office to smaller quarters to reduce the rent and began using an answering machine instead of an answering service. After implementing several cost cutting measures, the treasury is now growing at $350.00 per month and the district is considering the development of a reserve fund of $5000.00, which is about four month's worth of expenses. Several groups responded to the World Service Office, donating literature to Russian groups at a cost of $19.00 per shipment. The Public Information chairman was busy providing speakers to local schools and community colleges, and in the Adopt-a-Library program. We also celebrated at our special events, the Holiday Celebration and the Day in Al-Anon in May.

In 1993, Richard reported that the district had 41 meetings, 31 of which were evening meetings and ten of which were daytime meetings. Unity, diversity and flexibility continue to be encouraged rather than the confining simplicity of uniformity. Some meetings do follow the more narrow focus of the effect of the alcoholic, while others discuss the more open topics of abandonment, enmeshment, relationship difficulties, child abuse, molestation, incest, religious intolerance, the effect of the codependent's behavior on the family situation and the dysfunctional family itself. The Holiday Potluck was very successful both from an economic viewpoint and from the perspective of friendship, growth and healing.

There were some preliminary discussions with District 25 about working together in some areas or even coming back together as one district. While there was no opposition to this, neither was there any push to move forward with them.

One of our large Al-Anon Adult Children meetings was having problems for a long time. There was much gossip and criticism and traditions consistently being violated. Many in the district offered encouragement and support as the problems surfaced at the district, but we tried to stay out of the storm. Attendance dropped. The meeting was unable to take care of itself and finally closed. Some members were bitter and some sad. We are grieving the loss.

In 1996, Laurie R. shared. "There are now 36 meetings in the district, including two Alateen meetings. Our newest meeting began two weeks ago. It format is to discuss the new book, *How Al-Anon Works*[4]. The district continues to be registered as an Information Service, so we maintain a telephone line for incoming calls, a meeting schedule and a literature depot. In July we had our third annual expanded Day in Al-Anon. We flew in Bob L.[5] from Round Rock, TX as our main speaker. We have had continued success with this event. Everyone has a wonderful day of fellowship and it has been a successful fundraiser for our district. We have discontinued our Fall Luncheon. Instead we are planning two open Al-Anon meetings for the community, a first for our district. This is the third and final year of my term as district representative." At the 1996 election assembly, Laurie R. was elected to serve as Area Chairperson.

In 1999, Jennifer M. shared, "There are 37 meetings in the district, including two each of Alateen, Adult Child, Beginners, Women, three Spanish and one Parent. Unfortunately it has been a difficult year for Alateen and Institutions meetings. Our Beginners meeting at the Veteran's Administration Hospital closed. We learned that unless the institution itself is willing to support the meeting by requiring attendance of the families of their patients, the meeting does not survive. Two Alateen meetings closed. Either we can't get members to volunteer to become sponsors, or in the case of the other, we do have sponsors but can't get the parents to bring their children to the meeting. We have one Alateen meeting in the teen unit of a psychiatric hospital. It's a population in need and we love being there.

Our bimonthly meeting at a treatment center has blossomed into a regular weekly Beginners Meeting for the public and the families of the treatment center participants. Financially, the district is solid. The sixth Annual Relationships in Recovery Day in Al-Anon featured workshops. The spaghetti dinner was cooked by the teens. Butch and Larcine were our speakers. We were able to send the spaghetti-cooking teens to NoCAC, make donations to the World Service Office and to the area. This spring we were able to help NCWSA in their financial pinch with a donation of $1,000 and a loan of $1000.

In 2000, David P. was elected as district representative and also began to serve as the NCWSA Executive Committee Chairperson. In April, he resigned to pursue an educational opportunity in Florida and Laurie R. was elected to serve the remainder of his term as district representative.

District 25

In February 1985 Cathy C., the new District 25 representative, and Peggy P., the District 12 Representative, presented the division of District 12 into two districts to the assembly, which approved the change. District meetings continued to meet on the third Monday of the month at the South San Francisco Library. The district provided phone service with an answering machine in a member's home and kept the literature depot in another member's home. In 1991, the literature depot was moved to a Public Storage room. A telephone answering service was hired to take phone numbers of newcomers. Members who volunteer for Teleservice picked up the calls daily. Calls are returned. Literature and a meeting list are mailed to the caller. In 1997, the literature for the district was moved back to a member's home. In 2000, district meetings are held on the second Monday of each month at 7:00 P.M. in the Geneva Room at the Broadmoor Presbyterian Church, 377 87th Street, Daly City.

In her 1996 report, Claude P. shares that there is a pool of 31 volunteers who are available to staff the Teleservice phone line. Each volunteer is available one day each month with a one-year commitment. If someone can't do their service they contact an alternate to take over. The literature depot has a new location and the inventory has been trimmed, both resulting in substantial savings. The district was able to do this because some of the members have been willing to come forward and do service. Our groups also supported the district.

Notes

[1] *Wife of the Alcoholic* was a pamphlet printed by the Utah Foundation and carried on the AFG Headquarters, Inc. price list until 1976.

[2] *Alcoholism, A Merry-Go-Round named Denial,* P-3, is published by AFG Headquarters, Inc.

[3] The "3 Deadly Enemies" also known as "The Obstacles to Success" can be found in the pamphlet *Alcoholism, the Family Disease*, P-4, published by AFG Headquarters, Inc.

[4] *How Al-Anon Works*, B-25, is published by AFG Headquarters, Inc.

[5] Bob L. was originally from Riverside, CA. He and his wife, Goldeen, now live in Sun City, CA.

16

District 14

When the area divided in 1963, the district remained the same size as it had been previously and included the cities of Antioch, Concord, Danville, El Cerrito, Martinez, Orinda, Pittsburg, Richmond, Tracy, San Pablo, Pleasant Hill and Walnut Creek and was called District VII. In 1982, when the area changed the district numbering, this district became district 14. At some time in the 1980's, El Cerrito, Richmond and San Pablo moved to district 26. Today, the district has 43 groups meeting each week, including two Alateen meetings, both in Antioch, and two Spanish Speaking meetings, both in Pittsburg.

In 1974, the district was meeting monthly to discuss several opportunities. Among them was the meeting at juvenile hall. Groups would rotate their attendance at this H & I meeting. The district decided to keep its newspaper ad as it reads. The treasurer reported a balance of $42.79. Tillie K. from Sacramento and Carl G. from Carson City, NV spoke at the August 1974 open meeting. This open meeting has been in existence since 1970. The delegate, Bonnie H., spoke at the Day in Al-Anon in September and the registration fee was $1.00. Sales of "Easy Does It" buttons were profitable. Arci provided educational materials to a community group that was writing a manual about community resources. A Public Information letter was mailed to the schools. Members of Alateen from Concord, Pittsburg and Pleasant Hill attended the Young People's AA meeting and also the Alateen meeting in Juvenile Hall on a monthly basis.

In 1975, the district report says, "Nine years ago, there was only one group active at the district and area level. Today, there are 12 group representatives, 4 Alateen groups, 3 Hospital and Institutions groups, including one in Juvenile Hall. There is a Preteen meeting being sponsored by two young AA men, to their credit."[1]

In 1977 an advisory committee recommended that an Information Service be formed and that it be called the "Al-Anon Service Center." It would serve as "an avenue for local public information and institutional work as recommended in the

pamphlet." A decision as to whether the service center would carry "only Conference Approved Literature" or if "other generally acceptable literature should be
stocked" was deferred until the Board of Directors was named. They discussed the
merits of incorporating as a nonprofit corporation. They were also responsible for
the local newsletter. They recommended the appointment of a visitation committee, which would visit every group and explain the functions of the service center.

Because the space being used at the AA service office was no longer available,
the new office for the service center was opened at 1359 Locust St, Walnut Creek.
"It was noted that the district now has enough money to cover the expenses of the
Al-Anon H & I Conference in Fresno in May, 1978. No further special donations
are requested. AA has been notified about the new Al-Anon phone number." AA
continued to refer calls to Al-Anon and continued to print the Al-Anon meetings
in their schedule.

By 1981, the district had 42 meetings, including 9 Alateen meeting. There is
a Spiritual Breakfast meeting at a local restaurant with a breakfast-speaker-discus-
sion format that lasts three to four hours. The Men's Stag Group celebrated its 6th
anniversary this year. They have had visitors from Los Angeles and Ohio.

A long time member shares

A long time member, Kathleen D. shares about the beginnings of Martinez Tuesday Night Kaiser AFG and the Alateen meeting in Martinez. "I moved to Martinez,
California, in May 1978. Shortly after arriving I found Al-Anon meetings in Concord (the Al-Anon Fellowship on East St.) and in Pleasant Hill (Hillcrest Congregational meetings on Sundays and Thursdays). But none in Martinez. So I was
delighted when I read a few weeks later in a Kaiser Permanente member newsletter
that AA and Al-Anon were meeting on Tuesday evenings at the newly opened
Kaiser-Martinez facility about two miles from my home. This meeting was in
existence in 1974.

"When I arrived the following Tuesday, I found the AA meeting in a conference room in the hospital, but no Al-Anon. I sat through the meeting, and
afterwards found a Kaiser janitor and asked if he had seen any other community groups meeting in other buildings. I said, " Probably a few women, perhaps carrying small blue books." He said he saw no one, but led me from the
hospital to a couple of other buildings checking conference rooms. So the
next Tuesday I went back, again went to the AA meeting and this time asked
the secretary who was the group's contact at Kaiser. It was Dr. Levy from the
Psychiatry department.

"I placed a call to the doctor the next day, and found out he had just transferred to Martinez from the Richmond Kaiser. He had called AA and asked that
they start a meeting at the new Martinez facility. He thought Al-Anon always met
with AA—as indeed they did in 1978—but he did not know Al-Anon and AA
were separate organizations. So I volunteered to find someone from Al-Anon in

Contra Costa County who could perhaps start a group that would meet at the same time as the AA meeting."

"The next week I left early for the East Street meeting. I asked the people who had arrived early if anyone knew someone from Martinez who attended Al-Anon. Several remembered Evelyn, "but she hasn't been coming lately." I asked if they thought she would mind a phone call from someone, and could I look through the meeting sign-in books. Not a problem. So I paged through the books. Martinez at that time had only two phone prefixes, so Martinez numbers were easy to spot.

"This is where I'm sure a Higher Power was working. Just as I jubilantly found an 'Evelyn' with a 228 prefix, the door opened and someone said, 'Here she is!' She and I talked after that meeting. There used to be meetings in Martinez, but the group had folded. And yes, she was interested in another meeting closer to home. She thought Martinez might be such a small town, the population then was about 20,000, that people might be afraid to attend an Al-Anon meeting in their home-town.

"By the end of the summer Evelyn and I were meeting, and by fall Helen G. joined us. She registered the group on December 14, 1978 as the Martinez Kaiser Hospital (Smokeless) AFG. We were the first non-smoking meeting in the County, and for many years we were the only one. Kaiser Permanente Hospital was not set up to accept room rental from the group. We decided to give literature in lieu of rent to the facility. Through the years we put out thousands of pieces, primarily the three Twenty Questions lists. In the beginning we wrote district 14's information number on each piece, then we stamped them, and later Lorraine[2] printed up small computer labels that we'd stick on each item. We paid particular attention to stocking the emergency room racks between Thanksgiving and New Years. At Christmas we gave books, videos, or Forum subscriptions to the Kaiser Hospital.

"On the registration card sent to the World Service Office, Helen listed herself as the group's secretary and also as the treasurer, noting the positions remained combined until we were full grown. Evelyn also volunteered to be our group representative. Elaine B. was perhaps the third member of the group, and then one night in 1979, Lorraine B. showed up. From a display put out by Helen on a downtown Martinez bulletin board she'd picked up the small public information leaflet, *Are You Concerned about Someone's Drinking?*[3] Lorraine carried the leaflet until it was tattered, and then one Tuesday night, she drove up to Martinez Kaiser Hospital to find us. Just as I had found the AA group in the conference room, so did she. But this time Helen's husband Jerry spotted her, asked if she was looking for Al-Anon, and walked her down the long hall to where we were meeting. Years later she told of her surprise to see us—perhaps four, five or six of us—sitting around a hospital room—sitting on the beds!

"In those first few years the hospital kept moving us around. The room Lorraine entered later was made into a small meeting room. When we outgrew that, we asked for and were assigned a larger room. But always, in those early years, the Kaiser administrators kept us near the in-patient Psychiatry ward. And almost every week a nurse would walk a patient down to our meeting, and we would have a chance to see how real 'insanity or death' could be for the family member of an alcoholic.

"Lorraine and Evelyn both had teenagers they were concerned about, and they were taking turns driving their children to an Alateen meeting in Pleasant Hill. Rather soon they asked if I would start an Alateen meeting for their kids. I didn't think I had any qualifications, but they asked again and again, saying I was the only person they knew with any length of time in Al-Anon, and that, to them, seemed to be the prerequisite for a sponsor. So we started an Alateen meeting every other week. I was working full time by then, and felt I needed a recovery meeting for myself on the alternate weeks. With time I told the kids I'd be available any Tuesday they could show up. We continued for several years, growing at one time to nearly 15 regular Alateens, including a group of 5 or 6 who came from Benicia to find us."

"Around 1990 Lorraine asked if I would help her start the Sunday night SOS meeting in Martinez. She felt weekends were particularly hard for families of alcoholics. Again it was a one-hour meeting so people could meet 'At Arms Length' as Evelyn B. used to say at the Tuesday Smokeless meetings. Lorraine always said 'SOS' could mean whatever an individual chose. To some of us it became Sanity on Sunday, or Serenity on Sunday. To others, just 'Help! I'm drowning, and I need a meeting.'"

Groups Share

Linda A. shares about her own meeting[4]. "In June 1980 I went to my first Al-Anon meeting in Concord at St. Bonaventure Church on a Monday night at 7:30 PM. To the best of my knowledge, Alex and Rita McG. started it over 20 years ago. She has since passed away. I was surprised how many people (approximately 200) were there for the same reason as I. They had people come in from different meetings to chair. It was really nice to hear so many different stories, but yet we all had the same common bond. Today the meeting is still being held in the same room and is still going strong, with a lot of newcomers and regulars still coming after all these years. In 2000, there are about 25 to 30 people who attend and there's a lot of good sharing. We do a step study the first Monday of the month. On the remaining Mondays, group members chair by signing up. Sometimes someone from another group comes to chair. God has really watched over this meeting through the years."

The woman who started the Monday One Day At A Time Study Group in Clayton[5] shared. "There wasn't a meeting in the area that worked in my time frame, so I started one. The one thing I like about the group is we pick a topic out of the index from the ODAT.[6] Everyone reads a page on the topic and then talks. It has been wonderful for beginners who find it hard to talk at first."

Another lady from one of my night meetings, an old timer, shared, "The Clayton Monday Morning (10:30 AM) Al-Anon Group held its first meeting on

Jan. 4, 1999. To our knowledge, it was the first ODAT Study Group in this area. We only use the ODAT book. It might be interesting to think of it this way. The meeting could be considered a spin-off of the San Bernardino Thursday Morning Al-Anon Group (the first in San Bernardino, going back about 35 years), since the Clayton meeting was started by a long-time member of the San Bernardino group, She had 24 years in the San Bernardino group when she moved to this area in 1997."

Two members of the Walnut Creek 9:30 AM Friday group (#52347), Linda B. and Simon, started the "How Al-Anon Works" group (#60524) on September 5, 1996. Linda B. was strongly motivated to start a new group that would strictly adhere to using Al-Anon conference approved literature at all times. She asked Simon, who was fairly new to Al-Anon, to team up with her and he enthusiastically agreed.

Simon had been involved in youth work at Our Savior Church, remembered the Creekside Room and thought it would make a wonderful place for an Al-Anon meeting. The room is to the west side of the church and looks out towards trees and a creek and the sound of the water flowing over a waterfall is calming and tranquil. Church representatives had already rented the room to AA for a Saturday evening meeting. They offered the room to Al-Anon for $20 per month.

The group format uses the Al-Anon guideline *Starting An Al-Anon Group*[7] (G12). That format has not changed in the four years since the group's inception other than the closing prayer. In July 2000, the group changed the closing prayer to the Al-Anon declaration, following the group founders' intent to only use Al-Anon approved material.

The group today has 20 regular attendees with several members who are sponsors. The meeting is a one-hour meeting but many members stay after for a half-hour or more for continued program discussion. And so every Wednesday morning at 9:00 AM, miracles begin in the Creekside Room.

Notes

[1] *12 Stepper*, June 1975.

[2] Lorraine continued to print labels for us after she was bedridden with cancer. She produced the last batch just a few weeks before she died.

[3] *Are You Concerned about Someone's Drinking*, M-1 is a small leaflet published by Al-Anon Family Group Headquarters, Inc.

[4] WSO Group # 796.

[5] WSO Group # 063327.

[6] *One Day at a Time in Al-Anon*, B-6 published by Al-Anon Family Group Headquarters, Inc.

[7] *Starting An Al-Anon Group*, G-12, is published by Al-Anon Family Group Headquarters, Inc.

17

Districts 15, 16, 17 and 26

Prior to 1963, the California area was divided into 19 districts. What became District VIII was then called District 6 and 19. The north border of District 6 was the San Pablo Bay, included San Pablo, Richmond, Pittsburgh and Concord. Its southern border was the Oakland-Alameda line. District 19's border extended south to the Santa Clara County line to include Fremont.

In 1963 the boundaries of the Northern California area's districts were changed as a result of the division of California1 into two areas. At that time Districts 6 and 19 were combined as District VIII. The "new" District VIII eventually divided into what are now approximately the boundaries of Districts 15, 16, 17 and 26. Cities listed on the 1964 area map include Alameda, Oakland, Hayward, Albany, Fremont and Livermore. We believe that the East Bay, including Berkeley, was part of the district in 1964 based on the earlier map. In 1982, District VIII divided into three, numbered 8a, which included El Sobrante to Hayward, 8b, which included San Ramon to Livermore and 8c, which included the cities south of Hayward (Fremont, Union City and Newark) to the Santa Clara County line. That same year, the area renumbered the districts and the districts became 15, 16 and 17. In 1988, the new District 15 divided again, placing El Sobrante to Berkeley in the new District 26, and leaving the cities from Oakland to Hayward with the current number 15. During the remainder of this report, there will be many references to Intergroup as well as district. While there were district boundaries, an Intergroup also existed that provided local services for the district 15 until the district and Intergroup merged in 1983. There is a separate Intergroup that began to serve the needs of those in the south end of District VIII, long before any divisions occurred. It continues to operate in what is now District 17.

Very early groups

The earliest group for families known to exist in the district called itself the Adeline Nalano Group. They met every other Monday at Ruth C.'s home at 2831 Dohr Avenue in Berkeley. There is no indication whether this group responded to Lois' letter in May 1951. However, the group in Alameda did respond to the letter about the Traditions. Their vote to accept the Traditions was recorded on February 17, 1953.

The Park Street Group in Alameda held many meetings each week, including an Alateen meeting and a combined meeting with AA called the "Late Night Rap Group" that met at 10:30 PM on Saturday nights. Al-Anon meetings were listed in the Alcoholics Anonymous Meeting Directory. AA bought, stocked and sold Al-Anon literature, and AA accepted calls from those wanting Al-Anon meetings.

The San Leandro Group first met in 1955 on Tuesdays. Later on it changed its meeting night to Mondays. It spun off from the Diamond Link Group in Oakland to better serve Al-Anon members in the city of San Leandro. It continues to meet today on Monday each week.

Intergroup and District Offices and their functions

An Intergroup was formed that encompassed all the cities in the original District VIII. The group representatives of six groups, from Alameda, Dublin, Hayward, Oakland, San Leandro and San Lorenzo, met in April 1969 at the AA office on Opal Street in Oakland. When the Intergroup was formed, it included an Executive Committee consisting of the officers. It was in early 1972 that AA suggested that the Al-Anon Intergroup become self-supporting. AA asked Al-Anon to buy its own literature, find its own office and staff its own phone number. At the April 1972 meeting, the representatives agreed to call their office the "Al-Anon Information Center" and began looking for a location for the office. By October 1972, the Intergroup office opened. The groups held several fundraising events, breakfasts, buffets and a Christmas Boutique to pay for the expenses of the new answering service and the office. In early 1973, a note in the Newsletter indicated that they were also concerned about finding lower printing costs; "The blind will do copying for very little." Apparently, the cost of the office was a concern to some, because at the June 1973 meeting, a motion was recorded as a "unamouse (sic) vote to keep the office open."

In January 1974, the office rent increased to $67.00 and the Intergroup then found another office for $50.00 per month. After an answering service was obtained in 1974, the books and pamphlets were moved to the Literature Chairperson's garage and the office was closed. There was also a second office on Pendleton St, off Hegenberger, in Oakland.

Apparently, the Intergroup secretary became pessimistic in 1975. She reports in the minutes, "Al-Anon is going downhill." Another person was apparently concerned about the committee meetings themselves. He wrote, "A camel is just a horse designed by a committee".

This new office, located at 477 15th St in Oakland, was in a building that was set up to host non-profit organizations. The Intergroup office was there until the 1989 Loma Prieta earthquake destroyed the building. "We got a chance to be grateful. David, the last volunteer, left the building just 15 minutes before the 5:04 PM earthquake. Our Al-Anon literature, on which so much of our serenity depends at times, was saved—not a page was destroyed." "The building was cordoned off and access denied. On Monday October 23rd, occupants were suddenly given permission to go in and retrieve what we could. Nancy T., Olga R. and Lee went in and recovered District 15's entire stock amid cracked walls and crashing light fixtures. They packed everything except one bookcase, and loaded Lee's truck to remove our literature to Olga's garage. The physical effort of packing hundreds of books and pamphlets plus furniture is no small accomplishment." "None of us will ever forget where we were or what we felt, the cry, the fear. And we shouldn't. Neither should we forget, 'There but for the grace of God…' because it will be in the gratitude that our healing will be found."[2] Eventually, District 15 found a new office at 15287 Hesperian Blvd in San Leandro, where it continues to serve the district today.

Answering Services

In 1972, when AA suggested that the Al-Anon Intergroup become self-supporting, the Intergroup added a phone in the office and groups rotated the responsibility to supply people willing to take calls. The individual groups would also purchase literature that was mailed to the callers. In March, 1974, the minutes indicate that the office was not staffed at least 50% of the time, so the Intergroup found a professional answering service, the Hawthorne Company, to help. The cost of the service in 1974 was $25.00 per month for up to 65 calls and there was an additional cost of $0.20 per call above that amount. The answering service would answer the phone and patch the call to an Al-Anon person on a list provided by the Intergroup.

One problem discussed at the October 1977 Intergroup meeting was how to refer callers to outside organizations. "The group discussed giving out addresses and phone numbers of shelters and referring callers as Al-Anon members. We need to resolve whether we are offending other people or not and misusing shelters."[3] The minutes don't describe their solution.

Since the 1970's, calls made to AA by family members of alcoholics have been referred to our own published Al-Anon telephone number. Likewise all calls to the East Bay Al-Anon Intergroup from those who want to stop drinking, want detox information and who are ordered by the courts to Alcoholics Anonymous have been referred to AA's published phone number.

The district phone number is listed in the Yellow Pages under Alcohol Information and in the business listings. Al-Anon is listed two ways, both with the (-) dash and also spelled as Alanon, (for those who don't know how to spell the name).

Literature Services

Prior to 1972, the local AA Intergroups in Oakland, Hayward and Livermore, provided Al-Anon literature for the Al-Anon communities. When AA in Oakland asked Al-Anon to become self-supporting, they also donated the entire Al-Anon literature collection to the Al-Anon Intergroup on consignment with no deadline for repayment. By March 1974, the Hayward and Livermore AA Intergroups also stopped supplying Al-Anon literature. In 1974, the Al-Anon office was closed and Al-Anon literature was now stored and sold from a member's home. The criteria for the Literature Chairperson included "An Al-Anon member preferably with a sober alcoholic, responsible for keeping Al-Anon literature in the home." By 1976, the purchase of literature was such that the Intergroup could take advantage of quantity discounts. According to the minutes, "Olga suggested that intergroup wait until they needed $250.00 worth, to be able to buy literature in bulk."[4] Apparently AA still had some leftover Al-Anon literature in 1979, because they contacted the district representative, Wenche E., "regarding $245.00 of Al-Anon literature they have on hand. They are offering to sell us the literature for $191.00."[5]

Meetings and Lists

Al-Anon meetings were listed in the AA Meeting Directory as late as 1985. But the Al-Anon Intergroup began printing its own meeting list in 1977. This early list included 15 groups, including the A-7-A Al-Anon and Nalano Discussion, Al-Anon and 12 X 12 Study in Oakland, East Oakland, Island Al-Anon (this group met at 1828 Lincoln Ave), Alateen, Preteen, Al-Anon Study and New Hope in Alameda, Al-Anon and 12 X 12 Study in Hayward, and meetings in Dublin, San Leandro and San Lorenzo. A new Alateen group in San Lorenzo formed in 1976. In the late 1970's, several more new meetings formed. A letter was received asking to establish a "Young People's Al-Anon meeting for ages 18 to 25", and another asking to start a "Men's Stag" meeting. Intergroup offered each group the "standard" $5.00 to assist them. In 1979, the first group for Adult Children of Alcoholics began meeting, the first Lesbian group met on Tuesday's in Berkeley and a new Spanish group met at St. Bede's Church in Hayward.

Fund Raising Events

The Intergroup treasury had a balance of $127.38 in the middle of 1976. They often showed films at fundraising events in the 1970's, including showing "Lois' Story" several times while they rented it for a week, a "Film Festival" using films received from the library of the National Council on Alcoholism, such as, Father Martin's "Chalk Talk," "99 Bottles" and "Time for a Decision," where 70 to 80 members attended and the Intergroup collected $102.00. In December 1977, an Alateen sponsor developed a skit called "Garbage Game," which was used to promote Alateen. In 1978, "Gary B. announced a Pancake Breakfast, whose purpose is to raise money so that Alateens could attend the Southern California Alateen Conference (SCAC)." The Alameda and San Lorenzo Alateens hosted the breakfast at the Island AA Fellowship at 1828 Lincoln Avenue, Alameda. It occurred each month with (always) overcooked sausages and (occasionally) undercooked pancakes and with the (sometimes too much) help of Alateen sponsors. It helped to finance sending Alateen members to SCAC (Southern California Alateen Conference) until the NoCAC (Northern California Alateen Conference) was formed in 1978.

Skits

The Al-Anon members were and are very talented and enjoy creating skits. Since 1985, they wrote several skits to be presented at the Northern California area Conventions and Conferences. Performers included Ruth McG., Anne R., Olga R., Catherine H. and several other supporting characters. Members of the troupe came from every city in the district from Berkeley to Hayward. The skits often went "on the road" to other district events. These include "Miriam the Martyr,"[6] "The Steps, (with alien participation)," "The Journey to Joy" and "Miracles Happen."[7]

Public Outreach

As early as 1973, the Intergroup sent a letter to doctors in the district, letting them know of the existence of Al-Anon and Alateen and how these groups could help families of alcoholics. By 1976, a Hospitals and Institutions meeting was being held at the Oak Knoll Naval Hospital in Oakland where there was a treatment facility. This facility was instrumental in hosting several significant events. As well as encouraging Alcoholics Anonymous and Al-Anon Hospital and Institutions meetings at its facility, the hospital was active in recruiting AA, Al-Anon and Alateen participation in their own treatment program for military personnel. They often had programs for their doctors and nurses who would be dealing with alcoholics. Dr. Pursch was instrumental in developing these programs. He later became the guiding light in Southern California at the Betty Ford Treatment Center.

Al-Anon and Alateen members would share their own experiences with family members who had someone at the treatment center. They also focused on sharing with doctors and nurses, who were members of the helping professions. They related to describing the family's disease and provide invaluable help in these meetings. Early in 1976, Al-Anon members also attended a health fair. Later, Connie suggested that the district begin an annual H & I Conference.

Newsletters

A former district representative, Madelen L., established the first newsletter in January 1977. Among the items printed in that issue was a notice about a Speakers' Workshop in San Lorenzo and the 10th Annual Pacific Regional AA Service Assembly (PRAASA), which was held in March in Seattle, WA. A newsletter called *Newsletters* in the archives is dated April, 1982 and listed as Vol 1, No. 1. This name was changed in 1984 to *News Notes* and published regularly from January 1985 to 1993 and then occasionally until the April/June issue in 1998. A new editor began the *News Notes* again in July 1999. It has been regularly published since then. Early in the year 2000, the district worked with the NCWSA area Internet Committee to establish a web page at *http://www.ncwsa.org/d15/*. This web page currently includes the meeting list and a calendar of events.

District 16

LaVonne O. shares the following. "In 1980, I became the group representative for my home group. At that time I tried to get in touch with the district representative of District VIII of which my group was a part. After much research what I found there was no active DR in District VIII, but there was an Intergroup. I finally found where and when their Intergroup met and I went to the meeting. I met a woman named Dorothy from Castro Valley. I explained to her that I wanted our group to be represented at the district level and wanted to know how to contact the area. I had read about the structure of Al-Anon in the Handbooks. Dorothy contacted several other Al-Anon members from District VIII and asked them to attend a meeting so we could select a district representative and be represented at the area. At that meeting, I was elected DR of District VIII.

"Since I understood that a DR was supposed to attend all the meetings in his or her district at least once during the year, I attempted to do just that. However, at that time District VIII had 56 meetings. There was no way I could attend them all, so the same group of us met again and discussed dividing the district into manageable areas that a DR could represent. We sent a letter to all of the meetings asking them to attend a meeting in Dublin on August 22, 1981. Included in the invitation was our proposal to divide the district. I can't remember exactly how many were there, but I believe it was about 22 of us. I do remember that no one from the Fremont, Union City and Newark area attended. We decided to divide the district just as it was described earlier.

"I attended the election assembly in September 1981 and was elected Recording Secretary for the area. After I had been to the first area assembly and had a taste of what my new job entailed, I figured that was a big enough job and so I resigned as district representative in August of 1982 and my alternate became the DR.

"My home group 'Monday Night Dublin-San Ramon' began meeting before 1968, but how much before I have no idea. When I became DR in 1981, there were 4 meetings in the Dublin/Livermore area and none in Pleasanton. Before I resigned as DR we had increased to 6 meetings and the number of meetings were growing. We grew enough to host the election assembly in September 1984."

Some significant events in District 16

1. Suzie M. was instrumental in starting Al-Anon in the Tri Valley area in the 1970's.
2. The first organizational meeting for District 16 was held on August 22, 1981. The Tri-Valley Information Service was formed, Ruth K. was elected chairperson, and LaVonne O. was elected as district representative. Chris B. served as alternate district representative. In September 1981, the district established a PO Box, answering service and a bank account. The district meeting was held at 7:30 P.M., followed by Information Service meeting at 8:30 P.M.
3. The first Federal Correction Facility Al-Anon Institution meeting was started at the Pleasanton, California Prison on February 25, 1983 at 7:00 P.M. with Jackie C. as sponsor.
4. The first Day In Al-Anon was held on April 30, 1983.
5. A monthly Speaker meeting was started on October 14, 1983. It was held the 2nd Friday of the month at St.Claire's Episcopal Church, at Hopyard & Valley Trails in Pleasanton. Groups in the district took turns hosting the speaker meeting.
6. LaVonne O. was elected chairperson of Tri-Valley Information Service in July 1983. At this time, the district and the information service merged into one organization.
7. In January 1985, Gordy volunteered to write a newsletter for the district.
8. In October 20, 1987 the monthly speaker meeting started passing out Birthday coins for Al-Anon members.

District 17

In 1975, the cities of Fremont, Hayward, Livermore, Pleasanton and Dublin established their own Intergroup. Just as District 16 was formed in 1981 from the old District VIII, so was District 17. Its boundaries included the old "Five Cities" (Irvington, Warm Springs, Niles, Mission San Jose and Centerville districts), which are now Fremont, Union City and Newark. The district has FUN with the new initials of their cities, including sponsoring a FUN Day in Service in the fall of 2000. Several members share about their experiences in the district.

Dorcas' husband Bob, Dee C. and Margaret started the Five Cities meeting in 1961. DiAnn came shortly after, in 1963.

Florence P. started in Al-Anon in April 1968 at the Five Cities meeting. She came in as the result of her husband's drinking. When Joy C. called Florence to attend a meeting, her husband was already sober and a member of AA. She got Florence into service, including working with the answering service and the Intergroup, at that time in Alameda. In 1968, there were two meetings, Prince Of Peace and Five Cities, which had as many as 20 people in the room. The pamphlet *This is Al-Anon*[8] and the book *One Day At a Time in Al-Anon* (ODAT) were the first pieces of literature used.

When Nancy N. called Al-Anon, she spoke with the janitor at the AA office, so her first meeting was an AA meeting. She entered Al-Anon in January 1973 at the Tuesday meeting at the old Bus Depot on Peralta. Ten to twelve people attended her first meeting. It is a very old building, now an historical site, and the floor slanted to one side. This Tuesday meeting currently meets at the Baptist church in the Irvington district. She paid $3.50 for her first ODAT. Nancy also attended the Five Cities meeting on Thursday night and the Monday meeting at Washington Hospital. Nancy also worked on the answering service and in Intergroup.

Phyllis O. began in March 1975 at the Five Cities Group on both Tuesday and Thursday night. One was a Step meeting. She used the phone list and called Florence, who often drove her to the meeting. There were very few people at the Friday noon meeting on Bonde Way. Phyllis also remembers the Washington Hospital and Newark meetings.

Ruby had a taste of Al-Anon in Southern California in the sixties, but at that time, Al-Anon wasn't for her. By May 1979, her husband had been in and out of AA several times. She went to her first meeting at Prince of Peace Church, where there already were five or six members. Shortly after, she became the secretary and remained. Ruby worked at both the Intergroup and the answering service.

In 1978, Pat R. attended her first meeting in Newark. Grace, Meryna T., Pat B. and Gert O. were there at the time. Her Intergroup involvement began in 1979, which met at Florence's house.

In 1989, Delta D. attended her first meeting at the Thursday night Five Cities. It was a big meeting with 15 to 20 people in a little crowded room. The Washington Hospital group had a meeting on Monday at 8:00 PM with 20 to 40 and a newcomers meeting at 7:00 PM with 15 to 20, and a Wednesday Step Study meeting, chaired by Mary H. There were Alateen meetings going on at that time. The first man to attend meetings was Bob (Donna's husband). The Washington Hospital Group was the only place where men attended (Fred, Ralph and Pete). Five Cities celebrated anniversaries. The birthday meetings started as a speaker meeting at the Alano Club in Newark. Debbie I. was responsible for the birthday meeting. The birthday meeting moved to the Fremont Hospital. Intergroup still met in member's homes until they requested that the hospital accommodate the business meetings. The first Day in Al-Anon was held on May 1, 1993 with the theme: "A Life Preserver Button May Day—Higher Power."

In 1992 Debbie S. and Delta D. started Preteen and Alateen meetings at the Prince of Peace Lutheran Church. The meetings had been closed for about 2 years. As new sponsors they gathered information from other members that sponsored the meetings and sponsors in other districts. They found suitcases that had literature and guidelines for the Preteen and Alateen meetings. Delta sponsored Preteen and was a substitute Alateen sponsor for 4 years. The meetings were very small at first. As time went on the meetings got bigger and better. The Al-Anon Intergroup voted to support the Alateen groups by recommending that Al-Anon groups take a second collection for Alateen. This is used to assist in funding NoCAC scholarships and as a literature and rent fund. Preteens who come back regularly to the meeting are given an *Alateen—A Day at a Time*[9] book. There is an annual Alateen birthday party, where the members receive a birthday coin and an Alateen or Al-Anon book of their choice as part of the celebration. When there is a "fifth Tuesday" the Al-Anon and Alateen members share a joint meeting. The teens influenced the Al-Anon members to close with "Happys". The meetings continue in existence today and are very active.

Carol A. started in August 1989 because a marriage counselor recommended attendance at Al-Anon. She first attended the Five Cities group and also attended the Wednesday night Step Study and the Friday night meeting at Fremont Hospital. A local store, Creative Arts, designed the Al-Anon birthday chips. Teddy Bear chips were given to Alateen and Preteen. The Step Study Group gave chips for completing the steps. The chips used for the birthday meeting had a butterfly on one side and the numeric number symbolizing the year on the other. The chips used today are similar to the AA chips except that the Al-Anon chips have the Al-Anon symbol.

Jeanne E. began in October 1990 at the Tuesday night Prince of Peace meeting. She brought her grandson to Alateen with her. A week later she was the literature person. She attended her first conference in Modesto in April and brought back some of the books for the meeting. She remained literature person for some time. Finally another member volunteered so Jeanne could let go.

In 1998, Randy M brought together materials to start a web site for the district. This web site includes meeting locations, several pamphlets about Al-Anon and Alateen, links to recovery meetings and other Al-Anon web sites and their intergroup phone number. Quite attractive, it includes flying butterflies and walking footsteps. Today, the district has fifteen meetings, including an Alateen and a preteen Alateen meeting.

District 26

The decision to form a new District 26 by dividing District 15 was approved at the February 1988 Assembly. The District 26[10] territory included all the old District 15 borders north of Oakland-Berkeley line.

A long time member, Charli D. shared, "I became a member of Al-Anon in 1988, soon after the districts split. I attended one district meeting as group treasurer in 1989 or 90. At that time the district meetings were in the office wing of Calvary Presbyterian Church on Milvia Street in Berkeley. The office was one used by psychologists and counselors. Looking back through what records District 26 kept, there was correspondence with the area and District 15 referring to 'a place of our own.' District 26 incorporated in 1988 as 'District 26 AFG Information Services.'

"Until 1991, the Thursday afternoon AFG at Northbrae was fairly affluent with always a large financial reserve. After the Oakland[11] fire, many of the women who had attended that meeting moved to surrounding communities. For a while attendance was very low. Rent and bank fees reduced the reserve as the group's balance dipped below the cutoff for free checking. "I think the same may have happened to other groups, as the district was very lean financially by the time I started attending district meetings.

"I became a group representative in 1993 at the end of Angela H.'s term as DR and was present when Minerva was elected district representative. The 1994 Assembly was my first. The district was having a hard time filling positions, and attendance at the monthly meetings was low. I became Alternate DR and attended the May 1995 NCWSC[12] meeting in the DR's stead. Right after the Convention in July, she resigned and I attended the August NCWSC meeting as DR. On the way back from the assembly in 1995, Karen W. agreed to stand as alternate DR and was elected at our next district meeting."

By the beginning of 1996, Karen W. and Charli D. had contacted all the existing groups in District 26, removing ones from the meeting schedule that had not met in some time. The district decided to close the office. Instead they held the district meetings in the homes of members. Saving the rent was enough to get a two-mailbox voice mail system for the Information Service. Volunteers returned calls and send out meeting schedules. The district voted to make the Information Service their first priority, and to suspend having events and selling literature until sufficient energy and funds were available.

In 1993, the Day In Al-Anon held at the Calvary church was moderately attended, and did not break even financially. Charli D. volunteered to put the Day In Al-Anon together for the district. Minerva had booked Calvary's parish hall. It burned, but the district was able to book the Unitarian Church in Kensington. Art

B.[13] and his wife Sarah attended that one. Don R.[14] led one of the workshops. Again, it barely broke even. In 1995, Karen W. and Charli D., co-sponsors of the Young People United Alateen Group, and also serving as alternate and district representatives, planned a new type of event, at least new for the district. Instead of a "Day-In" it was an evening potluck, with speakers (again at the Unitarian Church in Kensington). Donations again did not quite cover expenses.

In 1997, with the Al-Anon Information Service running smoothly, Karen W. started focusing on public information and when the area coordinator resigned, took that position at the area level also. Unfortunately, Karen moved out of the district partway through her term. Rose de P., the alternate, became DR. by the first NCWSC meeting of 1999. She brought enthusiasm and time in program. Group representatives became active and stepped in when Rose had to curtail her activity during rough spots in her pregnancy. District picnics were held in 1998 and 1999, and two workshops were held. The last picnic and workshop broke even or had a slight surplus financially. Now in 2000, Dan S. is district representative, all the officer positions are filled with people willing and enthusiastic about their jobs, and coordinators for Alateen, Institutions and Public Information are in place.

Notes

[1] The 1963 World Service Conference, effective with the new terms of delegate, approved the division of California into two areas January 1964.

[2] District 15 *Newsletter*, p 5, sharing by Terry P.

[3] District VIII (now 15) minutes, October 1977.

[4] The WSO began providing volume discounts some time after 1970.

[5] District VIII (now 15) minutes, 1979

[6] Presented at the Oakland Northern California Al-Anon Conference, July 12, 1986.

[7] Presented at the El Cerrito Northern California Conference, June 1997.

[8] *This Is Al-Anon*, P-30, is published by AFG Headquarters, Inc.

[9] *Alateen—A Day at a Time*, B-10, published by AFG Headquarters, Inc.

[10] The dividing line is shown on the current map of the area.

[11] A fire devastated the Oakland Hills district, destroying over 3,000 homes. Many residents were elderly and moved away rather than wait for their homes to be rebuilt.

[12] The Northern California World Service Committee met four times each year, between Assemblies.

[13] Art B. was the delegate from 1994 to 1996.

[14] Don R. was the area treasurer.

18

Districts 18 and 27

At the end of 1952, the Modesto group was one of the eleven from Northern California listed with the World Service Office. On the 1964 map of the area, District IX included the area from Sacramento to Fresno, including the cities of Lodi, Tracy, Stockton, Sonora, Modesto and Merced. The World Service directory for that year included meetings in Merced and Modesto. In 1967, the World Service Office surveyed all the Alateen groups. The Modesto Alateen Group reported that the age range for their group was 9 to 13 years. This appears to be the earliest record of a preteen Alateen group in Northern California. Eleven years later, the area summary indicates that the district had grown to 13 groups, including one Alateen meeting. In 1982, when the area renumbered districts, this district became district 18. At their district meeting on July 25, 1993, the group representatives voted to divide the district. The division was affirmed at the 1993 area assembly.

District 18

In 1990, Frankie N. reported that the district included seven counties, Alpine, Calaveras, Mariposa, Merced, San Joaquin, Tuolomne and Stanislaus. There are two Intergroups in the district, one in Stockton and one in Modesto. The 46 adult groups, 13 Alateen groups and two Al-Anon Adult Child groups hold 115 meetings each week. They held a clergy workshop, two health fairs at local colleges and participated in an Alcohol Awareness Forum in Newman. There are newcomers meetings in Turlock, Modesto, French Camp and Lodi. The campout at French Camp was again very successful, and the Yosemite Campout was sold out again. Marty H. spoke at a Serenity Workshop. At the area election assembly in 1990, Frankie N. was elected area chairperson.

In 1992, two district committees were formed to divide the district. The two committees brought their ideas to the assembly in 1992. After much discussion, the motion makers tabled the motion to accept the new district. At the end of 1992, Frankie accepted a position in Utah and resigned as area chairperson. The following February, both committee chairpersons met with the acting area chairperson. They agreed to meet as a joint committee, worked out their differences and the assembly approved the division of District 18 and numbered the new District 27 in 1993. After the division, Deanna B. reported, "One of the most controversial issues last year was the splitting our district into two. I am pleased to announce that this was successfully accomplished. I would like to commend Linda W. and John R. for their diligent work and the fine example of Al-Anon at work as they visited each group."

The Modesto Information Service has provided at their request over 400 Newcomer packets to the Modesto police department. Police officers carry these packets in their patrol cars to give out as needed.

In 1996, Lynda W. reports, "The district consists of Stanislaus, Mariposa and Merced counties. There are 19 groups with 33 weekly meetings. We have Alateen meetings in Modesto, Ceres and Turlock, as well as meetings in five local high schools. The Public Information Coordinator just did her yearly mailing to all the schools in the district. Our answering service is doing well. We are able to keep the lines filled with volunteers. Our media representative is doing a good job of keeping our name and phone number in all the local newspapers and on the cable stations."

In 1999, the other Linda W. shared, "Lynda W. was a member of Al-Anon for over 22 years. She helped start many groups in our district and started the Information Service. She was a driving force in our district, and for those of you who knew her, she was a driving force wherever she went. She gave a lot to Al-Anon over the years and we are so grateful that she was a part of our lives. She will be missed, but she left a legacy like no other. And all the lives she touched, all the people that she encouraged into service carry that legacy into the future for her." Lynda W. was only 49 when she died. In 1999, the district now has 26 meetings, including two Alateen meetings, five more Alateen meetings in the high schools, and one Institutions meeting. There is even a meeting in Yosemite on the National Park grounds.

District 27

District 27 now covers Alpine, Calaveras, San Joaquin and Tuolomne counties. Three members stood for district representative, Cranston, Chris C. and Kathy G. Kathy was elected to be the first district representative and served through 1996. In her 1994 assembly report, Kathy G. noted that there were 27 groups that held 53 meetings. The district and the Delta Al-Anon Information Service cooperated in holding three Days-In-Al-Anon in March, May and September. The district participated in several health fairs. At the Red Ribbon Health Fair, attendance was 10,000 people. At the North East Community Center, 500 people attended and at the Su Salud Health Fair, there were 20,000 people who attended. The Answering Service Coordinator reported answering 40 to 60 phone calls each month. David R. became the district representative in 1997. He reported in 1999, "The district is large in area and varies in composition. It has 28 groups and about 55 meetings. In Tuolomne County, with a population of 52,800, there are three groups that hold six meetings weekly. Calaveras County, with a population of 38,250 also has three groups with three meetings each week. San Joaquin County, with a population of 545,000, has the balance of the groups and meetings. The groups support the district adequately with donations and our three fundraising activities are well attended. Our most urgent problem is getting members to stand for district offices."

19

District 19

Prior to 1963, the district that included Fresno and the surrounding area was labeled District 7. It included the cities of Bakersfield, even Barstow and the towns east of the Sierras along highway 395. When the California area divided in 1964, the district borders were adjusted, the district was renumbered District X and the borders still the same today. In 1982, when the area renumbered the districts, this district became District 19. The 1964 WSO Group Directory lists two groups in the district, one in Fresno, called Al-Anon No.1, and a second group in Hanford. In September 1975, the area group summary indicates that the district had 8 Al-Anon groups, one H & I group, and two Alateen groups. In 1979, Wanda A. became the district representative and Joyce M., the first Intergroup chairman. Daryl A. (a woman) wrote to the World Service Office and received the information necessary to get the district and Intergroup started. Daryl was very instrumental in getting everything organized. Shortly after, she moved away. She still lives elsewhere but comes back to visit from time to time.

Wanda A., a member since September 14, 1976, was a beloved active member of our district. Her passing on August 6, 1997 left a void that we have filled with wonderful memories of her. She served in many capacities from district representative to secretary and many offices in between. She served as the area treasurer from 1982 to 1984. She attended her first meeting to support a friend who was told to go to Al-Anon. Wanda stayed. While traveling with her, a member noted that invariably someone would come up to her and ask, "Aren't you Wanda A.?" Then they would proceed to tell her how she had touched their lives by sharing her experience, strength, and hope with them. Wanda seemed to be the contact point for people who had moved away or stopped coming to Al-Anon. They always stayed in touch with her. Carol H. shares, "She was the first Al-Anon I called after I got into the program. After listening to me go on for a while, she asked one question: Whom are you going to listen to—the alcoholic or your Higher Power?

I got shivers all over and was able, for the first time, to begin detaching from the insanity in my home and turning to God." Wanda had a great sense of humor. She often told the story of her husband using her car visit one of the local bars. The next day she couldn't find the *One Day At a Time in Al-Anon* books for her meeting. Her husband had handed them out the night before to people he felt needed Al-Anon. He never found sobriety, but he was a trusted servant in his own way. She never stopped loving him. "I mostly remember that she loved all of us, and she loved Al-Anon."

Newsletter of 1979

The first issue[1] of the District X newsletter was called *Newsletter*. Later on, the newsletter changed its name to *Alanews*. Some excerpts from this first issue are, "In early 1975, the Fresno district had only 3 meetings. Today (in 1979) the district now has 17 meetings in Fresno and the outlying areas, at least one for every day or night. The 24-hour answering service is celebrating its 1st anniversary on January 31st 1980. There are 52 active persons on the service to take calls at a designated time each week. In September 1977, the district began putting at least two ads per month, on Saturdays, in the local paper, the Fresno Bee. 'And these ads do get results. Ask any newcomer.' The Fresno Intergroup purchased 5 Public Service Announcements from the World Service Office and began distribution to TV stations in November 1978. The Intergroup sold necklaces and key chains with the Serenity Prayer, bumper stickers with 'Easy Does It' and two sizes of napkins with the Serenity Prayer. These are just some of the ways your Intergroup has been raising money for public service, the answering service, literature, etc." "Joyce M. worked tirelessly in sewing, cutting and selling book covers to raise money for Intergroup."

District X hosted the Al-Anon and AA Conference[2] in March 1980. District 19 hosted the 1st & 3rd All-State Conferences[3], both of which were held in Fresno,

Carol H. shares, "I started a *Meeting on Wheels* for shut-in Al-Anons. It was called Alatrip. Our Motto was: 'You call, we haul.' I don't remember the year we began, but it was sometime in the 80's. It wasn't a replacement for people to go to a meeting—just a short-term deal. Our first Alatrip was for a young mother who had a baby boy two days earlier. Within two weeks she and her baby were again attending meetings on a regular basis."

A Group shares

Trish M. shares that the Brentwood Friday night[4] meeting started about 1993. "The meeting was held in a church in Brentwood but had very little early participation. After about 6 months of meetings with only 2 people attending a wonderful lady named Juanita decided she would open her home on Friday evenings for a meeting. This way no one would have to sit in a cold or hot church waiting for new members. Juanita was the secretary. The group held the meeting in her dining room. She always had good coffee and delicious refreshments. Gradually the meeting grew and everyone took turns chairing. When Juanita was on vacation she gave someone the key so the meetings were held in her home even when she was out of town. I started attending the meetings in 1995 and loved going because it was so cozy. Juanita was like a mother hen to anyone who came. About 1997 Juanita and her husband moved out of state.

"At this point Joannie and I took over the meeting and moved it to the Methodist church in Brentwood. Juanita gave us her coffee pot to get us started. I have since turned over the secretary and treasurer positions to new members. Many members think that this meeting is just like a functional family; when we need new officers, everyone volunteers and just help out. It is the home meeting to many Al-Anon members. Today in 2000, attendance ranges anywhere from two to 16 people, and we usually have 1 to 3 men. We welcome everyone to our group."

District Representatives share

Betty B., finishing her term as the district representative, noted that the district had 80 Al-Anon and Alateen meetings. A one-day yard sale netted over $750.00 for the treasury. Each month at the district meeting, the groups participated in a one-hour presentation and question and answer period on an area of service. The literature depot adds 10% to the price of literature to cover the shipping costs and for the literature used at beginners meetings. At the August meeting, the district elected Betty's son, Steve B., an Alateen group representative, as their new district representative. Betty B. was elected in 1993 to serve the remainder of the term as area chairperson and also as the new area chairperson for the 1994 to 1996 term.

Illa H. shared that the district covers the counties of Fresno, Kings, Tulare and Madera. There are 70 meetings in the district, of which 33 are in Fresno and the 37 remaining meetings are in the valley towns. These include six Alateen meetings and one preteen meeting. In May, we had a very successful Day in Al-Anon picnic, and in June, a spaghetti dinner with a donation drawing. We heard three Alateens speak. We also hosted the 1992 California Statewide Convention.

By 1996, the number of meetings declined to 65. The district Bylaws Committee completed its work on the bylaws and distributed them to the groups for ratification. The Institutions Coordinator took an Al-Anon panel into the Pleasant Valley prison in Coalinga. Other panels are planned for the Women's Prison at Chowchilla and for the Kaiser Permanente Hospital. The district voted to create a "Non-English" Coordinator position. Carmen M. from Reedley was elected to this position.

In 1999, Beverly Anne S. reported that there were 62 groups in the district, seven of which are Spanish Speaking. There are four Alateen groups and one school-based group. The Alateen members did some serious fundraising to attend No-

CAC. With bake sales, car washes and other items, they raised funs for ten teens to attend. Officers and coordinators have begun a series of visits to groups outside of Fresno.

Notes

[1] While undated, it is fairly certain that this newsletter was published in the fall of 1979.

[2] The Northern California Council of AA and the area Al-Anon Assembly cosponsored this tri-annual AA Conference with Al-Anon participation.

[3] The California All-State conference alternated between Fresno and Bakersfield.

[4] WSO Group no. 45996.

20

Districts 20, 21, 22 and SCV Intergroup

Early AA Influence in Santa Clara County

San Jose AA Group One began meeting on August 13, 1941. At their Labor Day Barbeque in Menlo Park, 74 adults and 22 children attended. It was common at this time for the family to meet with the AA members, so we can presume that many of the adults were non-alcoholics. In the photograph, it appears that there are about 25 women present.

During a trip to the west coast, Bill W. and his wife Lois spoke on November 26, 1943 at the San Jose AA meeting held in the Montgomery Hotel and the following week on December 2nd at the Palo Alto group. Bill and Lois also stayed with Dave D. and his wife for Thanksgiving in Palo Alto.[1] Lois customarily spoke a few words about the needs of the family at these meetings and also met privately with the wives.

The Trinity AA Group held its first meeting in November 1946 at the Trinity Episcopal Church at 2nd and St John Streets. It was an open meeting in which non-alcoholic family and friends were encouraged to participate. Potluck dinners and other after-meeting socials were common. The group met at another location for a few years and returned to the church in the early fifties, changing its name back to the Trinity Group.

In 1946 an AA Men's Group was formed because the jealous wives of some AA members objected to women in the meetings, Oddly enough, this group met at the Woman's Club at 75 South 11th Street. At his meetings with AA's in 1943 and again in 1948, Bill W. mentioned the need for some central organization. What grew out of that was the Northern California and Nevada Council of Alcoholics Anonymous. Shortly afterwards the Northern California Council of Alcoholics Anonymous (NCCAA) formed. George S., from Loomis joined the Sacramento non-alcoholic group in Sacramento in 1949. In 1952 he was elected chairman of the Northern California Al-Anon Council, which provided Al-Anon support to the NCCAA Conferences. Shortly afterwards, he moved to San Jose for about five years.

Another open AA group met in Cambrian at the Methodist church on the corner of Gunsten and Wyrick. In 1978, this AA group moved to St. Christopher's school on Curtner Avenue, as did the companion Al-Anon and Alateen group.

In March 1961, the NCCAA held its conference in San Jose with Ebby T. as the Saturday night speaker. AA and mostly Al-Anon members made the refreshments. It included 2,500 sandwiches and coffee for the 3,000 attendees.

Early Al-Anon presence

In October 1950, the San Jose group called itself the Alano-Mrs Group. It had fifty members and met on San Carlos St. The first secretary was Melba W., and Gerrie R. became the next secretary. When Lois W. and Anne B. wrote to the 87 known non-alcoholic groups, this group received her letter. We don't know if they replied. In early 1953, another letter from the Al-Anon Clearing House to the groups asked whether they would accept the Traditions as presented to them. While the number of groups who responded was low, the San Jose Group answered the letter and accepted the Traditions.

Organizing Al-Anon in the County

Early Al-Anon members supported the Northern California Al-Anon Council by electing delegates, attending the conferences and generally supporting their husbands in AA. Even though most of the Al-Anon members were women, John F. of San Jose was elected to the position of district committeeman of District 8 before 1963. His 1963 report is extensively quoted elsewhere in this history. In 1963, the Northern California Al-Anon Council invited an Alateen group representative from the San Jose Alateen Group to be a member of the Council. The WSO also asked this group for input to the Alateen portion of the 1965 AA International Convention held in Toronto. In 1964, when the area divided, the new District XI formed, which included all of Santa Clara County. There were eight groups in the district, three each in San Jose and Santa Clara, and one each in Saratoga and Sunnyvale.

The groups formed an Intergroup to serve the local public information needs. Lynn G. recalls that she was asked to speak about Al-Anon at the San Jose Women's Club luncheon. She took the time to inform the organizers at the Women's Club that no pictures of her could be placed into their newsletter and that it was important to not announce her last name, using the anonymity of the program as her reason. The *San Jose Mercury News* announced the event and used her full name and her topic, Al-Anon. Even in the Women's Club newsletter, she was pictured prominently and quoted by full name in their newsletter.

By 1975, the district had 38 meetings in the county, including six Alateen groups and one Institutions group. The Intergroup met at the welfare building on Younger Street in San Jose, the same location as the AA Intergroup. The AA Intergroup sold Al-Anon literature until 1977, when Al-Anon volunteers took on the task. Larue had the stacks of literature on her back porch in Los Gatos for several years.

Santa Clara Valley Intergroup Offices

In early 1980, Intergroup rented an office at a school on Radoyka Avenue in Sunnyvale. This is where they stocked and sold the literature and held their monthly meetings. For a short while they rented the space to a new Al-Anon meeting, the Joy of Living Group. The group left after a few months because the number of members couldn't fit into the room. In May 1985 Intergroup moved to Room 44 at the Campbell Community Center. The Jump Aboard AFG also used this large room. This group held meetings every night of the week, sometimes more than one each day. For this, they paid about 1/2 of the total rent.

In 1991, the rent for Room 44 was substantially increased. The Jump Aboard Al-Anon group didn't want to pay their part of the increase in rent and moved to a nearby office building on Rincon Avenue. Intergroup opted for a much smaller room, Q-83, and did all their business from that room. There was no room for meetings, so their monthly meeting and meetings of various committees were held in one of several rooms provided by the Community Center management. As the funds at Intergroup increased, they then rented the adjacent room, Q-82. This is used as a small meeting room and provides additional space for archives and business records.

Sales Taxes and Incorporation

In 1986, Intergroup officers became aware that they had not collected or paid the state sales taxes or filed corporate tax returns on their business of selling literature. Bob J. and Art B. headed a committee to decide how to proceed. After determining the amount of literature sold since the Intergroup was formed, they visited the Franchise Tax Board and "confessed" Intergroup's mistake. Working with the state official, who made suggestions about how to report the amount in a way that would reduce the penalties, the committee received a sales tax permit and paid back taxes and penalties of about $6,000.00. They also proposed a set of Bylaws for the Intergroup and filed for incorporation and non-profit status with the state and federal governments.

Meeting Directories

Intergroup became responsible to print Al-Anon meeting lists in 1977, but the AA meeting list continued to list the Al-Anon meetings until the early 1990's. The first meeting list was one standard sized page folded into three. In 1980, there were about 38 meetings listed. By 1988, there were over 100 meetings in the county. The Intergroup went to a smaller stapled 28-page booklet. This format was more convenient to carry in a purse or suitcoat pocket. Over the years it has improved by including the list of Intergroup officers, district representatives, the area delegate and phone numbers for nearby Al-Anon Information offices and the World Service Office. In the early 1990's, the groups began listing their WSO number next to their name, providing continuity for the groups when district representatives rotated out of their positions. The 2000 meeting directory shows there are 96 meetings hosted by 78 groups. These include four Alateen and one preteen meeting, 13 Spanish meetings including one Spanish Alateen meeting.

Insurance Needs

Intergroup purchased liability and theft insurance for their literature inventory and for their officers. Churches and other meeting facilities began to require that Al-Anon groups provide this insurance for their own meeting locations. Intergroup responded to the groups around 1987 by providing a codicil to their own policy to groups who wished to have this insurance. The cost was reasonable, about $30.00 per year.

Fund-Raising

Intergroup has held periodic events to support the functioning of this service arm. In the summer of 1980, the speaker was Elsa C. whose husband founded and led one of the first AA meetings in Southern California. Elsa C. herself opened the second Al-Anon meeting in Southern California, at her home in Laguna Beach in the 1940s'.

Jacqueline N. shared, "Our first Special Events Day was a tremendous success. All the district representatives attended, as did several past delegates and the present delegate. A panel of long timers from the beginning of Al-Anon in the valley attended and shared their memories. Another 124 members attended. We all listened to the sharing from our guest speakers. The hugging booth created an atmosphere of friendship and love. The $500.00 profit was used for Alateen."

Louise M. shared in 1999, "Our special event was a huge success, with a total registration of 138. Jim's deep-fried turkey was the hit of the lunch. A quilt made by our members was won by a long-time member, Helen L. After expenses, the event netted $1,400 and we also sold $400.00 of literature."

A former Intergroup chairperson shares what he tried to do at the yearly fundraiser when he served. He felt the barrier between the groups with adult children focus and those who were what he calls "mainstream". "In order to break down this barrier between the topics covered at ACA meetings and those welcomed at mainstream Al-Anon meetings, I co-hosted a day in Al-Anon. We invited guest speakers to talk specifically about sex, money, abuse of power, sexual abuse, and co-dependency, and we advertised the topics ahead of time. We had an astounding turnout, over 600 people attended."

Teleservice

Emily P., the NCWSA Liaison, reports, "Our Pac Bell Voice Mail is working well and seems to be a happy addition in 1996. The Teleservice Coordinator is in touch with members of our Spanish Speaking groups to add Spanish to the Voice Mail."

Public Information

Peggy C., the Public Information Coordinator around 1980, recently shared, "Some years ago I was asked to serve as the Public Information/Speaker List Coordinator. I happened to be good friends with the AA Speaker Coordinator serving AA's Intergroup. We were getting very few requests then for Al-Anon speakers at schools. We set up a strong committee and made a valiant effort to contact appropriate people at the high schools in the Santa Clara Valley. But we needed more help. AA was receiving many requests from schools for speakers, so my friend offered to suggest to the callers that they might want an Al-Anon and Alateen speaker, too. We couldn't believe the positive response from this very simple act. If they said they would like to have speakers from Al-Anon and/or Alateen she would give them my phone number as the Al-Anon contact. We got so many requests that I had to start recruiting speakers. I did this by putting on speaker workshops using guidelines from WSO. The workshops were great fun and we all learned so much. It was one of the Alateens in attendance who, after much pontificating by those of us who 'knew everything,' then asked 'What exactly is it that we want to let them know?' This is what we came up with:

> "1. If you have a problem with your own use of alcohol, call this number for Alcoholics Anonymous.
> "2. If you are concerned about someone else's drinking, or, if one or more of your parents is alcoholic, call this number for Al-Anon and Alateen.

"We would write these things on the blackboard with the appropriate telephone numbers, tell our story and leave time for questions. It was amazing to watch the questions change year to year as the teens in high schools became more and more aware of alcoholism and its effects on the family."

In 1996, the PI Committee donated literature to twelve libraries, visited "at risk" kids at juvenile hall in San Benito County and took literature to Santa Clara High School.

Dividing into Districts 20, 21 and 22

In 1979, the district divided into three new districts. These were called 11-A, 11-B and 11-C until 1982 when the area renumbered the districts as Districts 20, 21 and 22 to reduce confusion caused by the alphabet. Intergroup continued to provide local support for the districts. The districts supported the delegate, brought issues to the attention of the delegate and to reported back to the groups on the solutions offered by the World Service Office and the area.

District 20

This district covers the northern part of the former District XI, and includes Los Altos, Saratoga, Sunnyvale, Cupertino, and parts of San Jose. Lillian P. reported, "We started a Speakers Meeting held on the 4th Friday of the even month. These meetings have added a new dimension to our program. They are useful in helping members qualify for the area's Conference Speaker's list. In 1993, the district had 22 meetings, including one Alateen and one preteen meeting. At the May district meeting, the group representatives discussed the participation of two groups in an outside enterprise. After a long discussion, the GRs voted 14 to 2, to not recognize these two groups within District 20."

Joan W. shared, "This year (1999) we decided to study the Twelve Concepts of Service from our service manual and from the *Paths to Recovery* book. Our discussions have been spirited and teach us how to apply these concepts in our groups, district, area and our home and professional lives. At our annual Day in Al-Anon, the KISS (Keep It Simple Sisters) delighted everyone with songs and a skit on Teleservice that I brought back from Australia."

District 21

This district covers the central part of the former District XI, and includes the central part of San Jose, Campbell and Milpitas. Art B. recalls when he attended his first assembly in 1981. "When we arrived at the election assembly in Sacramento, the delegate-chairperson, Faun L. discovered that several districts didn't have representatives. She believed that all the districts present needed district representatives, because they were the only persons eligible to serve as a delegate or area officer. Rather than continue, she recessed the assembly and asked all the districts without representation to elect one. Our district, 11-B, was one of those.

The six of us caucused. Two candidates emerged, Peggy K. and Laurie M. Peggy K. was elected as the district representative and Laurie as the alternate. We then returned to the assembly and voted our consciences for those who stood for office." Apparently, Carolyn H. had been DR at the time of the division, so Peggy served out the remainder of the year. Laurie M. became the DR and Art B. was elected as alternate. When Laurie resigned to go to school outside the area in 1992, Art served the remainder of that term and was elected to a full term of his own.

The district decided to hold its first speaker's meeting during this period. The first speaker was Carol A. from Lemoore and also the area secretary. The following year, Abe E., an Al-Anon member from San Fernando Valley in Southern California spoke. This man was in his 80's and told how in the early 1940's he would tell the AA meeting he attended that he was an alcoholic so he could hear and use their recovery for himself. He was especially noted for being able to recite the 12 Steps backwards, from 12 to 1.

In 1993, Jenni H. reported, "we created a group representative handbook to give to each new GR that comes to a district meeting, or when a group asks for information about the district. Our GRs are working on detailed job descriptions and experiences we have had over our term in office. This is to give the new officers a better chance to get to know their jobs better." The district was comprised of 24 Al-Anon meetings, including 2 Alateen and three Spanish groups. In 1996, Jenni H. shared, "Because of the success of our yearly speakers meeting, we were able to contribute to the World Service Office moving fund. The district voted to establish a fund for new meeting startups. The fund is used to encourage the growth of new meetings in the valley and offer them assistance in their first month's rent or their first literature order. Stepping down from being the district representative for the past five years is hard for me to do, but I know it is a necessity. I now have more patience, more friends, more tolerance and more joy. In other words, I have grown."

District 22

District 22 is located in southern Santa Clara County, reaching from Los Gatos in the west to Mt. Hamilton in the east, and stretching south from San Jose along the communities of Coyote, Morgan Hill, San Martin and Gilroy. In 1990 Michael L. reported that their 5th Al-Anon Day in Service is popular. It is traditionally held on the only non-football weekend in January. The district also sponsored an Adopt-A-Library project, where groups offer to adopt a library. The district donated one of the Al-Anon books, the group donated another book and the Santa Clara Valley Intergroup provided the pamphlets through their Public Information program. The district had 42 groups, including five Alateen and two Ala-Child groups.

Carol L. reported in 1993, "The past three years hold some wonderful memories of what we accomplished and what fun we had. It included three Days in Service, two potluck meetings, a writer's workshop, donations of literature to Russia and an interesting project making garlic heads as mementos to send to Peggy C. when she went to the World Service Conference."

Sue B. shared in 1996, "This year our difficulties are in getting and keeping good Alateen sponsors. We added two events to our agenda this year, a Couples Speaker Meeting and Dance, and a Couples Speaker Meeting and Pot Luck. Both were very successful. I thank all of you for your love and support. About this time next year, I'll be casting off the dock lines and heading south to other countries to carry the message."

Cathy F. shared in 2000. "The Day In Service is held each January on the Saturday of the weekend prior to the Super Bowl. For the past several years the Day In Service has been graced by the creative endeavors of Vicki H. and her 'Vanna,' Michele M. Humbly named 'The Game Show,' Vicki incorporated a fun, and, at times, hysterical game using Al-Anon principles, slogans, Conference Approved Literature including translations and caricatures of notable national and local members. Prizes are hand-made bookmarks bearing slogans, or other similar tokens. We were saddened that our beloved Peggy C., our past district representative and area delegate, died on August 18, 2000. In January, she was still with us at our Day In Service. We had a large turnout with over two hundred people celebrating the new millennium and service. Our 15th annual Day In Service will be held on January 20, 2001. In keeping with the World Service Office's theme of celebrating 50 years of Al-Anon, the event's theme is 'Through the Years.' Our featured speaker is Peggy K., a long-timer from San Jose, who will share about 45 of those 50 years. We will also have panel speakers comprised of our past district representatives.

"District meetings currently combine business aspects with a coordinator from Santa Clara Valley Intergroup speaking about his or her particular area of outreach. We also had several interesting discussions regarding the proposed reorganization of Northern California World Service Area (WSO structural model), and the potential for a permanent office for the area. As a new district representative, I enjoyed the experience early in this year of traveling to all of the groups. The rooms were large or small; the people many or few; the setting day or night; and the facility in the middle of a bustling city or in a quiet neighborhood. The same loving atmosphere of serenity and friendship perfused each and every meeting."

In 2000, there were 26 active groups, including 2 Alateen and 1 pre-teen group. This number included the Serenity Alateen Group, formed in early 2000 in response to Operation Alateen.

Note

[1] *50 Years: A Celebration of Sobriety*. A program presented at the San Jose Cultural Center, June 29, 1991.

21

Districts 23 and 24

The Early Days

On the 1964 map of the area, the new District XII included Santa Cruz County and those counties south of Santa Cruz. The World Service Directory for that year included meetings in Salinas, Santa Cruz and Watsonville. Eleven years later, the area summary indicated that the district had grown to 13 meetings. Ray C. of San Jose revealed that he attended his first meeting in Salinas in 1951. Stella, another long time member, shared that she attended meetings as early as 1949. She is proud of the fact that her husband started an AA meeting in their home that "included the women" in the mudflats section of Watsonville in 1949. "They felt the need for both partners to be able to share their feelings." This meeting continued to exist until the 1970's. The first Al-Anon meeting began in Aromas. She attended Al-Anon meetings in Salinas and in Watsonville during this period. She was proud that she attended an Al-Anon function in the area that featured Lois W., co-founder of Al-Anon. Her own daughter began to attend an Alateen meeting in the late 1950's. In 1968, there was an Alatot meeting established in Boulder Creek. This group of 8 to 12-year-old youngsters even printed a newsletter, *The Alatot Trailblazer*, describing their purpose and activities.

District 23

In 1983, District 23 divided and the two parts were numbered 23 and 24. District 23 covered the north part of the old district and included Santa Cruz, Watsonville, Freedom and Hollister. Mary A.-T. became the first Alateen Coordinator after the division. In the months in between district meetings, the district held Al-Anon/Alateen Connection workshops. There were five or six Alateen meetings then, each of which had two sponsors, one male and one female. The teens held a series of fundraisers, including "bowl-athons" to finance their attendance at NoCAC. Seven drivers took almost 30 teens to the conference, caravanning both ways. The funds raised were sufficient to reimburse the scholarship fund as well as their parents' advance.

In 1988, the district began working towards incorporation. They rented an office, a literature depot and obtained their first answering machine. In 1990, the district completed their work and applied for non-profit status with both the IRS and the state. They found that the work required to maintain records, to meet IRS deadlines and other paperwork were more than their members were interested in keeping up. In 1993, the district started the process of unincorporating and dismantling the literature depot. In the process, they distributed all their funds to other non-profit entities. They sent 40% to the World Service Office, 30% to the WSO moving fund and 20% to NCWSA. All the literature in the depot was donated to the Santa Clara Valley AFG Intergroup. The distribution occurred just before the annual Craft Faire in December. While funds were tight for a short while, the groups responded well. Rod J. and Chris, the publishers, reported that the district newsletter, *Way and Pace*, was nine years old. It contained lots of member sharings and was published every other month. Stella, with 42 years in the program, was the featured speaker in October.

By 1990, the district had 40 meetings, including four with an Al-Anon with Alcoholic Parents focus, four Alateen meetings and 2 Institutions meetings. The meetings in the district held several speaker meetings and four service workshops. Election of the district officers was handled by appointing a nominating committee in February. They conducted a service workshop in July and presented a slate of candidates. At the meeting, open nominations were added. All the positions and alternates were filled. The district Craft Fair was again the fundraiser. The major moneymaker is the raffle of a district created quilt. 35 Al-Anon members participated in making the quilt. The Watsonville meetings held their annual spaghetti feed and the teens had a potluck picnic. The teens also spoke at schools and participated in the Alcoholism and Drug Addiction conference with the South county teachers. When the film, *When a Man Loves a Woman*, was showing, Kurt R. received permission to place Al-Anon posters at the theaters.[1]

Chris M., the district representative for the 1997-1999 term reported, "Great things continue to happen with Public Information. Carrie has been very active with contacting TV stations with the new video clips. It is wonderful seeing our message getting out to the public. Our new answering service finished its first year, including voice mail. We receive more than 200 calls per month and we mail about a dozen meeting lists to newcomers. This year the district took a careful look at a prudent reserve fund. Members are excited about our first Ice Cream Social and Talent Show in 1999. Alateen is still growing with enthusiasm and the word is spreading. The Alateen Coordinator, Dottie has spoken to several counselors and school officials throughout the county. "Who knows! Maybe some day we'll have Alateen meetings in all our schools."

Harlan H., the next district representative, talked up the idea of various events highlighting the 50th anniversary of Al-Anon. Stella, a long time member who started in 1949, was interviewed for the history book. In 2000, the district has 30 meetings, including three Spanish, one Alateen, one Adult Child, one Men's and one Institutions meeting

History of some groups

In 1987, Dee V., Chris and Mary A.-T. met to form the first Santa Cruz Gay and Lesbian Group. The meeting was listed as the Tuesday Night AFG (Gay and Lesbian oriented) and they agreed they would welcome anyone who came, regardless of orientation. "Some expressed difficulty referring to 'Him' in the Steps and Traditions", but in line with the Traditions and Concepts, they agreed not to change the wording of the steps. This group had between 40 and 60 in attendance. By 1987, the group wanted more of an Al-Anon focus and changed its format to studying literature, and changed its name to the Tuesday Night Literature AFG. It met at the Gateway school building behind the Grace Methodist church at Cayuga and Soquel Avenue. Another group was formed and met on Thursday night to handle the overflow.

The first Adult With Alcoholic Parents meeting began in 1983 at the Calvary Episcopal church at Center and Lincoln Street in Santa Cruz. "It has grown so large (in 1987) that the walls are bulging."

Gayle F., who was the Institutions Coordinator, started an Institutions meeting at the Janus Recovery Center at the center's request, where an AA group was already meeting. The Institutions meeting grew and included 12 to 15 regular members. At some point the group decided to change the focus toward a regular Al-Anon meeting. In 1985, the recovery center, noting that they wanted to refer spouses and families of alcoholics to a meeting with an Institutions format, found that they needed the space for other activities. Shortly after the Institutions meeting was formed, an Alateen meeting opened. The Alateen meeting was composed mostly of preteens, but it maintained an Alateen focus. Both the Al-Anon and Alateen meeting disbanded in 1985. In spite of this, Gayle F. spearheaded the formation of another Al-Anon group at the Janus Recovery facility, this time at 3:00 PM on a weekend afternoon. This group remained when the other closed. But in 1987, the recovery center needed the room, so the group moved to the Dominican Education Center on Soquel Drive.

A dual member saw the need for another Al-Anon meeting where members could go and learn more about the family disease. This noon meeting began on May 1, 1984 and met at the Villa San Carlos Community Room at 2500 Soquel Drive. It took a little time to "settle in". During the summer, a lunch program was in effect. The meetings were held at a table in the hall outside the Villa's office, because the office was closed between noon and 1:00 PM. The villa was a very large Housing and Urban Development apartment complex. They really wanted Al-Anon there. They were very cooperative in moving tables into the hall for us. Rob, a dual member, was the first group representative. He attended a district meeting and came back with the news that the meeting couldn't call itself a "Double winner" meeting any longer. The group renamed itself the Tuesday Noon AFG (with no dual member orientation). It is a large meeting (in 1987) with 20 to 25 in attendance. The time has changed to avoid interference with the summer lunch program. The group had met around two tables, but now there is a homier setting because we sit in couches grouped together. The meeting is informal. There is no chairperson. Whoever feels the need to speak first sets the topic for the meeting. All the Traditions are followed and children are allowed to be present.

In 1984, the Alateen group had a large attendance of members younger than 12. The Alateen group began a preteen Alateen meeting at the Church of Christ church, 637 Pacheco in Santa Cruz. They stressed that this was not a babysitting service, but those in attendance would read the same material as the Alateen group. Sponsors of the group included Gayle F., Marilyn, Mary A.-T., Sheila D. and Martha. In the fall of 1987, this group, along with the Beginner's AFG, the regular AFG and the Alateen meeting moved to the Garfield Park Church on Errett Circle in West Santa Cruz. Shortly afterwards, the preteen meeting closed temporarily, even though there were 25 to 30 in attendance because there were no members willing to be sponsors.

The AA Fellowship Hall on Highway 9 in Ben Lomond called the district representative, Mary A.-T. in an attempt to open an Alateen meeting at their location. While Mary was trying to find someone to sponsor a meeting there, an AA member did start the Alateen meeting on January 7, 1985. One of the Alateens called Mary to let her know that their sponsor hadn't shown up for several weeks. Mary became the sponsor until Sally R. took the position of sponsor. Then Jim W. joined her. The meeting room was often crowded and smoky. A youth home began bringing their youngsters to the meeting. This was quite disruptive since the youngsters didn't want to be there. The meetings were almost vacant during the summers, but the group became crowded again during the school year. Some of the teens have gone into AA, but they remain loyal to their Alateen meeting and the sponsors.

In October 1987, some of the Alateens at the Ben Lomond meeting wanted a smoking meeting, so they formed the Living, Loving and Learning Alateen group on Thursday night. It meets at St John's Catholic Church on Highway 9 and Russell Street in Felton at 8:00 PM, the same time as the Al-Anon meeting. About 8 to 12 attend this meeting.

In 1990, Fred J., Gary S., and Martin S. decided that the time was ripe for a men's Al-Anon meeting in Santa Cruz. After a site was located, Gary S. served as the first secretary. The group participated on the panels of several Days in Al-Anon, presenting the viewpoint of men in Al-Anon. During the summer and fall, the group occasionally would meet at a Santa Cruz beach or at a Redwood grove in

Boulder Creek on a member's property; at these events, the group met early and cooked dinner over a fire before the meeting. It also held several campouts at Henry Cowell State Park in Felton. From its beginning, the group met at Grace Methodist Church in Santa Cruz—until this historic building burned down in October, 2000. Though this group has varied in attendance, the strong feeling of fellowship among the members has kept it going through times of such adversity.

District 24

District 24 is the southern part of the old District 23 and is comprised of Monterey County from Salinas to King City and north to Prunedale. This includes Monterey, Salinas, Seaside and Carmel. In 1990, there were 23 meetings seven days each week. This included three Spanish Speaking meetings and three Alateen meetings. One of the Alateen meetings was held in a high school and was a closed meeting.

In 1993, Auburn V., the new district representative, was unable to attend the assembly but sent a report. The district was mourning the death of their district representative, Todd K.

In 1996, Charmaine F., the district representative reported, "As a district we are making gains in our ability to give service back to Al-Anon. Two groups had "pot luck" meetings with AA and Al-Anon speakers. These were fundraisers to support the group representatives who attended the assembly. We have 18 meetings and one Alateen meeting. There are people interested in starting another Alateen meeting on the Monterey Peninsula. We now have meetings in King City, Big Sur and Castroville, all well supported. Our biggest Public Information event was an article in the Monterey County Herald about AA and Al-Anon. A local reporter interviewed several Al-Anon members and wrote about one of them in the article. The article also published the Al-Anon 20 questions[3] leaflet.

Notes

[1] This film was the story of the life of a man coping with alcoholism and included some recovery. The World Service Office provided technical help to the movie producers.

[2] The following information was taken from a history written in 1987.

[3] *Are You Troubled by Someone's Drinking? Al-Anon is for You*, S-17, is available from AFG Headquarters, Inc.

22

Calendar of Significant Events

1. September 1939: In Monterey, Mrs. Kellogg purchased the book, *Alcoholics Anonymous*, for her husband.
2. January 1941: First non-alcoholic group based on AA principles meets in Long Beach, California
3. June 1941: Non-alcoholic wife is elected first secretary of the first AA meeting in Oakland.
4. November 1943: Lois W. speaks to 85 wives of alcoholics in San Francisco.
5. September 11, 1945: A Non-Alcoholic Family Group, the San Francisco Family Club, in San Francisco was formed. This was the earliest non-alcoholic grouping Northern California that became an Al-Anon Family Group.
6. October 1946: Trinity AA Family Group (for both alcoholics and their spouses) started meeting in San Jose.
7. July 10, 1950: The first issue of the *Family Club Chronicle*, later named the *Family Forum*, was produced.
8. May 1951: Lois W. and Anne B. send a letter to approximately 87 non-alcoholic groups known to AA.
9. July 17, 1951: The Roseville AFG was the first Northern California group to register with the Al-Anon Clearinghouse.
10. December 14, 1952: In San Rafael, the Northern California Al-Anon Council was formed during the AA Northern California Conference of the same date.
11. April 14, 1953: The Sacramento Group was the first Northern California group to vote to accept the Traditions.
12. June 13, 1954: At the Northern California Conference the first meeting for teenagers of AA's was held at an AA Conference with Al-Anon participation.
13. 1954: Permission was given to the AFG Headquarters, Inc to use the *FAMILY FORUM* name, forerunner of the *FORUM*.
14. 1956: First letter written from Northern California to the WSO about meetings for teens.

15. 1957: First Alateen Group forms in Pasadena, CA.
16. July 1960: At the AA International Convention in Long Beach, CA, Al-Anon members approve a plan for an Annual Al-Anon World Service Conference.
17. April 21, 1961: First Al-Anon World Service Conference held in New York City, with Helen B. from CA attending.
18. 1963: Alateen representative accepted as part of the Northern California Al-Anon Council.
19. Fall 1963: First Area Al-Anon Assembly meets at Berkeley High School in Berkeley, chaired by John F.
20. January 1, 1964: California divides into two areas, as approved by the 1963 World Service Conference.
21. February 1966: Alateen workshop topic at the Northern California Conference is "Talking in the Meeting".
22. 1967: Modesto Alateen group reports that the age range of their group is 9 to 13 years.
23. 1968: Spanish "Latino" group is formed in San Francisco.
24. October 10, 1970: The Northern California Al-Anon Council and the Area Assembly merge into the Northern California World Service Area.
25. 1971: Name of District Committeeman changed to District Representative.
26. 1971: First Alateen Conference.
27. 1972: Faun L. began a speakers' list.
28. 1976: First Convencion Hispana in Los Angeles.
29. 1979: First Northern California Alateen Conference (NoCAC).
30. 1982: The districts renumbered from 1 to 23, eliminating letter designations.
31. February 25, 1983: Institutions meeting forms at the Federal Prison in Pleasanton.
32. July 19, 1983: Northern California World Service Area is incorporated and receives its non-profit 501(c)3 status.
33. 1986: NoCAC officially becomes part of the Northern California World Service Area.
34. 1987: Alateens begin publishing their own newsletter—the *Alateen Express*.
35. 1987: Convencion Hispana holds first Convention in Northern California in San Francisco.
36. 1987: First Spanish Speaking Coordinator elected to the Area Committee.
37. 1989: Delegate speaks at the Convención Hispana in Fresno.
38. 1993: Hispanic Intergroup formed.
39. 1994: Local Al-Anon member demonstrates an Al-Anon Web Site to the AFG Board Chairman.
40. 1996: Hispanic Intergroup opens its own office in South San Francisco.
41. October 1996: Hispanic Intergroup publishes their first monthly newsletter, *LA ANTORCHA*.
42. 1997: Area Web Site funded by NCWSA now on line.
43. 1998: First Diversity Day sponsored by NCWSA held in Berkeley, CA,
44. 2000: Hispanic Intergroup elects an Alateen Coordinator.

23

Area Officers, Coordinators, Committee Chairpersons, District Representatives

1961 to 1963			
Position	**Person**	**Position**	**Person**
Delegate	Helen B-R.	Treasurer	Jane W.
Alternate Delegate	Ann O.	Secretary	Priscilla C.
Chairperson	Al S.		
1964 to 1966			
Position	**Person**	**Position**	**Person**
Delegate	Ann O.	Secretary	Emylee M.
Chairperson	John F.	Map Committee	Alice S.
Treasurer	Virginia C.	News Editor	Emylee M.
District I	Ardath W.	District II	Bev A., Irma C.
District III	Leona D.	District IV	Donnalie W.
District V	April F.	District VI	Jan B.
District VII	Mildred A.	District VIII	Roberta C.
District IX	Kathy L. (R), Ruth W.	District X	Ada D.
District XI	Golda H.	District XII	Stella McG. (R), Judy W.
1967 to 1969			
Position	**Person**	**Position**	**Person**
Delegate	Muriel B.	Secretary	Judy W.
Alternate Delegate	Emylee M.	H & I	Lois E.
Chairperson	67 Ann O.	News Editor	Elsie V.
Treasurer	Maxine K.		
District I	Ardath W.	District II	Irma C.
District III	Leona D.	District IV	Donnalie W. (R), Judy W.
District V	Virginia W.	District VI	Marge B.
District VII	Mildred A.	District VIII	Roberta C. (R), Andy A.
District IX	Eleanor B.	District X	Briggs B.
District XI	Golda H.	District XII	Stella McG.

1970 to 1972

Position	Person	Position	Person
Delegate	Judy W.	Alateen	Estella E.
Alternate Delegate	Francis S. (R), Peggy K.	H & I	Marion W. (R), Ada D.
Chairperson	Muriel B.	News Editor	Irma C.
Treasurer	Jan B.	Public Relations	Irma C.
Secretary	Teresa R.		
District I	Ardath W.	District II	Thelma H.
District III	Mimi C.	District IV	Doris B.
District V	Bev W.	District VI	Virginia W.
District VII		District VIII	Madelen L. (R), Vera G.
District IX	Eleanor B., Edith C., Maxine K.	District X	
District XI	Bonnie H.	District XII	Ruth W.

1973 to 1975

Position	Person	Position	Person
Delegate	Bonnie H.	Alateen	Arci P.
Alternate Delegate	Irma C.	Speakers Bureau	Faun L.
Chairperson	Bonnie H.	H & I	Carolyn H.
Treasurer	Charlotte A.	12 Stepper	Irma C.
Secretary	Faun L.		
District I	Jan B.	District II-A	Jackie B.
		District II-B	Faun L.
District III	Nicholas H.	District IV	
District V	Betty W.	District VI	Charlotte A.
District VII	Marion W.	District VIII	Helen A.
District IX	Ada D.	District X	Margaret M.
District XI	Phoebe H.	District XII	

1976 to 1978

Position	Person	Position	Person
Delegate	Irma C.	Alateen	Rhona M.
Alternate Delegate	Faun L.		Arci P.
Chairperson	Irma C.	H & I	Peggy K.
Treasurer	Lois B.		Carolyn H.
Secretary	77 Phoebe H., 78 Betty S.	Literature	Ellen T., Jean McL.
Public Information	Elva B., Margaret M.		Bonnie H.
Alateen Rep	Tim H.	Newsletter	Marian W.
District I	Mary H.	District II-A	Thelma H.
		District II-B	Margaret M.
District III	Cathe C.	District IV	Betty S.
District V	Betty W., Delores N.	District VI	Lois B.
District VII	Roy M., Arci P.	District VIII	Connie R.-W., Chris F.
District IX	Margaret M.	District X	Bev S.
District XI	Phoebe H.	District XII	Emily D.

1979 to 1981

Position	Person	Position	Person
Delegate	Faun L.	H & I	Connie W.
Alternate Delegate	Jean McL.	Literature	Barbara L.
Chairperson	Lois B.	12 Stepper	Irma C.
Treasurer	Mary H.	Public Information	Emily DeA.
Recording Secretary	Phoebe H.	NoCAC Committee	81 Laura J.
Corresponding Secretary	Cathy A.	NoCAC Committee	80 Pat F.
Alateen	Rhona M.	NoCAC Committee	79 Tim H.
District I	Carol J.	District II-A	Pat C.
		District II-B	Lois C.
District III	Carol A., Nicholas H.	District IV-A	Charlotte L.
District IV-B	Margaret H.	District IV-C	Barbara L.
District IV-D		District IV-E	Shirley H.
District V	Midge B.	District VI	Joan M., Chris W., Beverly M.
District VII	Roy M., Evelyn K.	District VIII	Chris F., LaVonne O.
District IX	Yvonne A.	District X	Wanda A.
District XI-A	Jean McL.	District XI-B	Carolyn A., Peggy K.
District XI-C	Irene R.	District XII	Joan L.

1982 to 1984

Position	Person	Position	Person
Delegate	Jean McL.	Alateen	Marilyn R.
Alternate Delegate	Peggy C.	Archives	Faun L.
Chairperson	Barbara L.	Bylaws & Insurance	Betsy N.
Treasurer	Wanda A.	Conference	Cathy A.
Recording Secretary	LaVonne O.	Institutions	Louise K.
Corresponding Secretary	Jan W.-G.	Literature	Kay G.
NoCAC Committee	84 Rhonda R.	12 Stepper	Beverly M., Irma C.
NoCAC Committee	83 Dave A.	Public Information	Phoebe H.
NoCAC Committee	82 Cathy S.	Alateen Liaison	Rhonda R.
Regional Trustee	Irma C.		
District 1	Arlene H.	District 2	Betty C.
District 3	Lavon C.	District 4	Lisa B.
District 5	Herb J.	District 6	Meredith B.
District 7	Margaret H.	District 8	Earthel N.
District 9	Virgil G.	District 10	Shirley H.
District 11	Midge B.	District 12	Steve F.
District 13	Phyllis B.	District 14	Kathleen D.
District 15	Wenche E.	District 16	LaVonne O.
District 17	Joan B.	District 18	Kay L.
District 19	Jan W-G.	District 20	Kay G.
District 21	Laurie M., Art B.	District 22	Peggy C.
District 23	Mary A-T.	District 24	Lois D.

1985 to 1987

Position	Person	Position	Person
Delegate	Barbara L.	Alateen	Rhona M.
Alternate Delegate	Mary A.-T.	Alateen	Linda J. (R)

Position	Person	Position	Person
1985 to 1987			
Position	Person	Position	Person
Chairperson	LaVonne O.	Alateen	Marjorie F. (R)
Treasurer	Wenche E.	Archives	Jean McL.
Recording Secretary	Carol A.	Bylaws & Insurance	Edith K.
Corresponding Secretary	Jan W.-G., Kay L.	Conference	Marilyn K.
Statewide Convention	86 Phyllis A.	Institutions	Wanda A.
NoCAC Committee	87 Kevin H.	Literature	Janet S.
NoCAC Committee	86 Shanna G.	12 Stepper	Cathy A.
NoCAC Committee	85 Gilbert H.	Public Information	Midge B.
		Alateen Liaison	Shanna G., Gilbert H., Annette B.
District 1	Arlene H.	District 2	
District 3	Jackie B.	District 4	Marge B.
District 5	Toni C.	District 6	Meredith B.
District 7	Margaret H.	District 8	Rhona M.
District 9	Joyce S.	District 10	Barbara P.
District 11	Catherine Q.	District 12	Peggy P.
District 13	Beverly L.	District 14	Kathleen D.
District 15	Irene T.	District 16	Jacki C.
District 17	Pat R.	District 18	Marty H.
District 19	Carol A.	District 20	Phyllis A.
District 21	Art B.	District 22	Joan E.
District 23	Anna P.	District 24	Geri B., Charmaine F.
District 25	Cathy A.		

Position	Person	Position	Person
1988 to 1990			
Position	Person	Position	Person
Delegate	Mary A.-T.	Alateen	Cathy A.
Alternate Delegate	LaVonne O.	Archives	Barbara L.
Chairperson	Peggy C.	Bylaws & Insurance	Ginger P.
Treasurer	Art B.		Jan W.-G. (R)
Recording Secretary	Lee D.	Conference	Judy G.-M.
Corresponding Secretary	Kathleen D.		Lillian P. (R)
Executive Committee	89 Michael L.		Janet S. (R)
NoCAC Committee	90 Jennifer W.	Institutions	Meredith B.
	89 Bill G.		Gayle F. (R)
	88 Julie W.	Literature	Edith K.
Statewide Convention	89 Joyce K.	12 Stepper	Barbara P.
Spanish	Virginia T.		Bob J. (R)
Alateen Liaison	Lisa F.	Public Information	Marilyn R.
	Shanna G. (R)		
District 1	Fernanda R..	District 2	Glenn S.
District 3	Gretchen J., Irma C.	District 4	Laurie S.
District 5	Jan K.	District 6	Janice W.
District 7	Eileen J.	District 8	Rhona M.
District 9	Margaret G.	District 10	Bertha M.
District 11	Ginger P.	District 12	Alma C.
District 13	Fred S.	District 14	Jeanne B.

1988 to 1990			
Position	**Person**	**Position**	**Person**
District 15	Marilyn R.	District 16	Rosemary W.
District 17	Marilyn B.	District 18	Frankie N.
District 19	Betty B.	District 20	Lillian P.
District 21	Nathan C.	District 22	Michael L.
District 23	Rosa K.	District 24	Jeffrey P., Ann G.
District 25	Kay O.	District 26	Sandy McR., Minerva M.-F.

1991 to 1993			
Position	**Person**	**Position**	**Person**
Delegate	Peggy C.	Alateen	Laurie S.
Alternate Delegate	Art B.	Archives	LaVonne O.
Chairperson	Frankie N. (R, Jan 93).	Bylaws & Insurance	Kate M.
Chairperson (Jan 93)	Art B. (Acting) Betty B.	Conference	Judy G.-M.
Treasurer	Marilyn R.	Institutions	Rhona M.
Recording Secretary	Cathy C.	Literature	Crissy McA.
Corresponding Secretary	Ginger P.	12 Stepper	Dav G.
Executive Committee	93 Ari T.-F.	Public Information	Betty B.
Executive Committee	92 Curt R.	Non-English	Antonio M.
Executive Committee	91 Angela H.	Alateen Liaison	Lia B., (R) Mike B.
NoCAC Committee	93 Dylan H.	Statewide Convention	92 Susan C.
NoCAC Committee	92 Lisa M.	Long Range Planning	Irma C.
NoCAC Committee	91 Kristina K.		
District 1	Shelah B.	District 2	Glenn S.
District 3	Sherri C., Terri C.	District 4	Nan M.
District 5	Gary P.	District 6	Janice W.
District 7	Norma J., Rissa S.	District 8	Betsy C.
District 9	Vern P.	District 10	Anita G.
District 11	Linda J.	District 12	Ari T-F.
District 13	Richard	District 14	Don R.
District 15	Tracey C.	District 16	Vic A.
District 17	Mary H.	District 18	Deanna B.
District 19	Steve B.	District 20	Curt R.
District 21	Judd L., Jenni H.	District 22	Carol L.
District 23	Davis T., Gary S.	District 24	Auburn V.
District 25	Priscilla N.	District 26	Angela H.

1994 to 1996			
Position	**Person**	**Position**	**Person**
Delegate	Art B.	Alateen	Vic A.
Alternate Delegate	Cathy C.	Archives	Curt R. (R), Carol H.
Chairperson	Betty B.	Bylaws & Insurance	Becky H..
Treasurer	Don R. (R), Frankie N.	Convention	Crissy McA. (R)
Recording Secretary	Marilyn R.		Vicki S.
Corresponding Secretary	Ari T.-F.	Institutions	Debbie M.
Executive Committee	95 Sharon G.		Rose R. (R)
Executive Committee	94 Gary S.	Literature	Jennifer W.

1994 to 1996			
Position	**Person**	**Position**	**Person**
NoCAC Committee	96 Carrie T.	12 Stepper	Vern P.
NoCAC Committee	95 Jessica B.	Public Information	Dav G.
NoCAC Committee	94 Monica S.	Non-English	Carmen M.
Convention Chairperson	96 Joan W.	Alateen Liaison	Tomasina R.
Convention Chairperson	95 Dav G.	Alateen Liaison	Andy B. (R)
Convention Chairperson	94 LaVonne O.	Alateen Liaison	Heather S. (R)
Regional Trustee	Mary A.-T.		
District 1	Keri R.	District 2	Mary S.
District 3	Jackie B.	District 4	Linda J., Dwight B..
District 5	Ellie C.	District 6	Chris W.
District 7	Nancy W.	District 8	Brenda A.
District 9	Carol K.	District 10	Connie F.
District 11	Cordie T.	District 12	John S.
District 13	Laurie S.	District 14	Sharon G.
District 15	Peter T.	District 16	Robert K.
District 17	Elizabeth K.	District 18	Lynda W.
District 19	Illa H.	District 20	Judi M.
District 21	Jenni H.	District 22	Susan B.
District 23	Gary S.	District 24	Wendy L.
District 25	Claude P.	District 26	Charli D.
District 27	Kathy G.		

1997 to 1999			
Position	**Person**	**Position**	**Person**
Delegate	Cathy C.	Alateen	Julie W.
Alternate Delegate	Vern P. (R), Gary S.	Archives	Carol H.
Chairperson	Laurie R.	Bylaws & Insurance	Marilyn R.
Treasurer	Steve R.	Convention	98 Steve B.
Secretary	Charli D.		97 Kathy B. (R)
		Group Records	Sandi C.
Executive Committee	98 Vicki H.	Institutions	98 Emily P.
Executive Committee	97 John S.		97 Laurie S. (R)
NoCAC Committee	99 Jennifer S.-W.	Literature	Cathy F.
NoCAC Committee	98 Tomisina R.	12 Stepper	Connie F.
NoCAC Committee	97 Shawn A.	Public Information	99
Convention Chairperson	99 Carl S.		98 Karen W. (R)
Convention Chairperson	98 Sandi C.		97 Nancy W. (R)
Convention Chairperson	98 Cindy Mc. (R)	Non-English	Janice W.
Convention Chairperson	97 Marilyn R.	Alateen Liaison	98 Travis A.
At-Large Trustee	Mary A-T.		97 Todd S.
District 1	Miriam H.	District 2	
District 3	Irma C.	District 4	Dwight B.
District 5	Leilani P.	District 6	Chris W.
District 7	Donna F.	District 8	Brenda A.
District 9	Phyllis N.	District 10	Sande A.
District 11	Patsy G., Nils P.	District 12	Glynn D.
District 13	Jennifer M.	District 14	Fran McN.

1997 to 1999			
Position	**Person**	**Position**	**Person**
District 15	Dottie L.	District 16	Charne S.
District 17	Delta D.	District 18	Linda W.
District 19	Beverly Anne S.	District 20	Joan W.
District 21	Cecelia K.	District 22	Vicki H.
District 23	Chris M.	District 24	Lorrie H.
District 25		District 26	Roise De P.
District 27	David R.		

2000			
Position	**Person**	**Position**	**Person**
Delegate	Marilyn R.	Alateen	Jennifer F.
Alternate Delegate	Vic A.	Archives	Irma C.
Chairperson	Vicki H.	Bylaws & Insurance	Nils P., Yvonne T.
Treasurer	Janice W.	Convention	Steve B.
Secretary	Sandi C.	Group Records	Beverly Anne S.
Executive Committee	00 David P., Art B.	Institutions	Charli D.
NoCAC Committee	00 Christy H.	Literature	Mary Ann H.
Alateen Liaison	00 Travis A.	12 Stepper	Gary S.
Diversity	Gina R.	PI/CPC	Connie F.
District 1	Yvette L.	District 2	Nancy A.
District 3	Bruce H.	District 4	Sheilah K.
District 5	Rita McG.	District 6	Chris W.
District 7	Robert J.	District 8	
District 9	Carol K.	District 10	Sally B.
District 11	Galey S.	District 12	Tom K.
District 13	David P., Laurie R.	District 14	Jim S.
District 15	Jim W.	District 16	Ruth K.
District 17	Elaine McC.	District 18	Mary Ann H.
District 19	Beverly Anne S.	District 20	Edie D.
District 21	Gina R.	District 22	Cathy F.
District 23	Harlan H.	District 24	Sally R.
District 25	Jennifer J.	District 26	Dan S.
District 27			

The Twelve Steps, Traditions, and Concepts

THE TWELVE STEPS of Al-Anon[1]

1. We admitted we were powerless over alcohol—that our lives had become unmanageable.
2. Came to believe that a Power greater than ourselves could restore us to sanity.
3. Made a decision to turn our will and our lives over to the care of God *as we understood Him*.
4. Made a searching and fearless moral inventory of ourselves.
5. Admitted to God, to ourselves and to another human being the exact nature of our wrongs.
6. Were entirely ready to have God remove all these defects of character.
7. Humbly asked Him to remove our shortcomings.
8. Made a list of all persons we had harmed, and became willing to make amends to them all.
9. Made direct amends to such people wherever possible, except when to do so would injure them or others.
10. Continued to take personal inventory and when we were wrong promptly admitted it.
11. Sought through prayer and meditation to improve our conscious contact with God *as we understood Him*, praying only for knowledge of His will for us and the power to carry that out.
12. Having had a spiritual awakening as the result of these Steps, we tried to carry this message to others, and to practice these principles in all our affairs.

THE TWELVE TRADITIONS

1. Our common welfare should come first; personal progress for the greatest number depends upon unity.
2. For our group purpose there is but one authority—a loving God as He may express Himself in our group conscience. Our leaders are but trusted servants; they do not govern.
3. The relatives of alcoholics, when gathered together for mutual aid, may call themselves an Al-Anon Family Group, provided that, as a group, they have no other affiliation. The only requirement for membership is that there be a problem of alcoholism in a relative or friend.
4. Each group should be autonomous, except in matters affecting another group or Al-Anon or AA as a whole.
5. Each Al-Anon Family Group has but one purpose: to help families of alcoholics. We do this by practicing the Twelve Steps of AA *ourselves*, by encouraging and understanding our alcoholic relatives, and by welcoming and giving comfort to families of alcoholics.
6. Our Al-Anon Family Groups ought never endorse, finance or lend our name to any outside enterprise, lest problems of money, property and prestige divert us from our primary spiritual aim. Although a separate entity, we should always cooperate with Alcoholics Anonymous.
7. Every Group ought to be fully self-supporting, declining outside contributions.
8. Al-Anon Twelfth-Step work should remain forever nonprofessional, but our service centers may employ special workers.
9. Our Groups, as such, ought never be organized; but we may create service boards or committees directly responsible to those they serve.
10. The Al-Anon Family Groups have no opinion on outside issues; hence our name ought never be drawn into public controversy.
11. Our public relations policy is based on attraction rather than promotion; we need always maintain personal anonymity at the level of press, radio, TV and films. We need guard with special care the anonymity of all AA members.
12. Anonymity is the spiritual foundation of all our Traditions, ever reminding us to place principles above personalities.

AL-ANON'S TWELVE CONCEPTS OF SERVICE

1. The ultimate responsibility and authority for Al-Anon world services belongs to the Al-Anon groups.
2. The Al-Anon Family Groups have delegated complete administrative and operational authority to their Conference and its service arms.
3. The Right of Decision makes effective leadership possible.

4. Participation is the key to harmony.
5. The Rights of Appeal and Petition protect minorities and assure that they be heard.
6. The Conference acknowledges the primary administrative responsibility of the trustees.
7. The trustees have legal rights while the rights of the Conference are traditional.
8. The Board of Trustees delegates full authority for routine management of the Al-Anon Headquarters to its executive committees.
9. Good personal leadership at all service levels is a necessity. In the field of world service, the Board of Trustees assumes the primary leadership.
10. Service responsibility is balanced by carefully defined service authority and double-headed management is avoided.
11. The World Service Office is composed of standing committees, executives and staff members.
12. The spiritual foundation for Al-Anon's world services is contained in the General Warranties of the Conference, Article 12 of the Charter.

General Warranties

In all its proceedings, the World Service Conference of Al-Anon shall observe the spirit of the traditions:

1. *that only sufficient operating funds, including an ample reserve, be its prudent financial principle;*
2. *that no Conference member shall be placed in unqualified authority over other members;*
3. *that all decisions be reached by discussion, vote and, whenever possible, by unanimity;*
4. *that no Conference action ever be personally punitive or an incitement to public controversy;*
5. *that though the Conference serves Al-Anon, it shall never perform any act of government; and that, like the fellowship of Al-Anon Family Groups which it serves, it shall always remain democratic in thought and action.*

Note

[1]The Steps and Traditions have been adapted from the Steps and Traditions of AA. *Al-Anon Alateen Service Manual 1998 - 2000*, © 1992. Steps, Traditions and Concepts are reprinted with permission of AFG Headquarters, Inc. The Steps and Traditions are reprinted with permission of AA World Services, Inc.